SPIRITUAL PRIVILEGES

YOU DIDN'T KNOW WERE YOURS

Donald G. Mostrom

INTERVARSITY PRESS
DOWNERS GROVE, ILLINOIS 60515

InterVarsity Press is the book-publishing division of Inter-Varsity Christian Fellowship, a student movement active on campus at hundreds of universities, colleges and schools of nursing. For information about local and regional activities, write IVCF, 233 Langdon St., Madison, WI 53703.

Scripture quotations marked NIV are from the Holy Bible, New International Version. Copyright © 1973, 1978, International Bible Society. Used by permission of Zondervan Bible Publishers.

Scripture quotations marked NASB are from New American Standard Bible, © The Lockman Foundation 1960, 1962, 1963, 1968, 1971, 1972, 1973, 1975, 1977.

Scripture quotations marked NEB are from The New English Bible. © The Delegates of the Oxford University Press and the Syndics of the Cambridge University Press 1961, 1970. Reprinted by permission.

Scripture quotations marked RSV are from the Revised Standard Version of the Bible, copyrighted 1946, 1952, 1971 by the Division of Christian Education of the National Council of the Churches of Christ in the U.S.A. and are used by permission. All rights reserved.

Distributed in Canada through InterVarsity Press, 860 Denison St., Unit 3, Markham, Ontario L3R 4H1, Canada.

Cover illustration: Roberta Polfus

ISBN 0-87784-982-X

Printed in the United States of America

Library of Congress Cataloging in Publication Data
Mostrom, Donald G.
    Spiritual privileges you didn't know were yours.

    1. Christian life—1960-   I. Title.
BV4501.2.M5954   1986   248.4   86-11383
ISBN 0-87784-982-X

17	16	15	14	13	12	11	10	9	8	7	6	5	4	3	2	1
99	98	97	96	95	94	93	92	91	90	89	88	87	86			

To Joyce:

*Since 1943 she has daily
unfolded for me
the deeper meaning of*

Love

Faithfulness

Companionship

Beauty

and a Heart for God.

No man was ever more blessed.

Preface

Malcolm Brown, George Silburn and I have been prayer partners since 1979. One day in our weekly half day of prayer together we began to discuss the significance of the new covenant as it is described in 2 Corinthians 3. It was obvious to us that this had something for our own lives and that it touched a large need in the church. This book is a direct result of that discussion and many further conversations.

As you read this book you will quickly become aware that this exploration carried me into much of the Scriptures. I have cited many passages, and I hope that you will catch some of the note of high respect I have for the integrity and authority of the Word of God. If you are to profit from such a survey of biblical teaching, I think you will need to have the same experience that we did—namely, to allow the Word to lead you into much prayer and personal application of its truth. Indeed, pray that the Holy Spirit, the mighty Teacher of truth, will open up the powerful significance of what he has written.

Although I have quoted from many versions of the Bible, this has not been done whimsically. All translations have strengths and weaknesses. When it seemed important to do so, I have sought to use the version that best catches the sense of the original language. When there is little at issue, I have used the New International Version because of its growing familiarity.

Many have helped generously with time and encouragement to make this book possible. Besides Malcolm Brown and George Silburn, several others read the manuscript and made helpful suggestions. Some did this with successive drafts. Among those who helped were James Brownson, William C. Brownson, Robert Elliott, James and Marion Huber, Ed Huff, Richard and Betty Lee Lovelace, Joyce Mostrom, Paul and Lisa Mostrom, and Carl Shank. Carl also guided me in some of my reading and research in covenant theology. I am indebted also to the editorial staff of InterVarsity Press, both for their friendship and their professional work.

A NEED FOR UNDERSTANDING

*T*he young man in my study was nineteen. He was tense and very much in earnest. With a mixture of fatalism and fervor he climaxed our conversation with these words: "Pastor, I appreciate what you are saying, but it really doesn't make any difference. I simply *must* have her!" Ken had tears in his eyes as he spoke, and I knew that his statement was as much an expression of helplessness as it was of rebellion, though there was, no doubt, some of both in what he said.

Ken, to all appearances, was a thoroughly committed Christian. Coming from a strong Christian home, he was well acquainted with the Bible and active in many church programs. He was a sensitive chap, with a strong sense of beauty, and there was something about him that made people respond lovingly to him.

Only a few knew how much Ken had been hurt in his past. Discipline in his home had been very strict and not always just. He loved his parents very much, but they came from a culture that forbade expressions of affection. He had not heard words of affirmation or appreciation from them, nor had he received expressions of love. He had been very insecure as a child, and this had been compounded by the strong favoritism his parents had shown toward a brother two years older. Ken had not gone to college after high school, because he simply didn't believe that he could. He did not know himself or his gifts.

Ken got a job at seventeen in a neighboring town and moved there, as a kind of first step toward breaking from his home and background. As a consequence of this move, he left his home church and joined ours. He immediately became a valuable asset to our program.

After a year Ken was elected to our Christian Ed. committee, and this was how he got to know Shelley. Shelley, on our staff as a paid Director of Christian Education, was a well-trained professional. She took a great deal of interest in the people with whom she worked, and we encouraged her to get the very best out of each member of her staffs and committees. Shelley was twenty-eight and a lovely Christian girl, as beautiful inwardly as she was outwardly. She immediately sensed the hurt and need that lay under the surface in Ken and felt challenged to help him overcome his insecurities. Under her encouraging leadership he began to find many of his hidden gifts and capacities. She affirmed him and showed kindness and appreciation toward him. Ken began to unfold like a flower. Shelley was pouring water on dry ground like no one before had done. It was not strange, really, that Ken fell deeply and hopelessly in love with Shelley. She epitomized everything that he needed and longed for. There was only one problem. Shelley was already married.

What Ken didn't know at first was how vulnerable Shelley was in this situation. Her husband was climbing the business ladder and giving it his undivided attention. He traveled a lot and paid little attention to his wife. He was an extremely self-sufficient person and showed no indication of personal need—for Shelley or anyone else. Ken's need for what she was supplying him and his gratitude to her were pouring water on her dry ground as well. She came to be as much in love with him as he was with her. They finally faced up to what had happened, and that's why Ken was in my study.

When Ken said to me, "Pastor, I *must* have her!" I was really in a bind. He knew as well as I did the Scriptures that said he couldn't have Shelley. His problem was not a lack of knowledge of God's laws, nor even of commitment to them. With his head he was thoroughly pursuaded of the rightness of them. But the more I said, "Ken, you can't do this thing," the more he said, "Pastor, I *must* do it." And his "must" was stronger than my "can't."

The situation I faced that night in my study was not unusual in today's church. Many counselors face it in one form or another with alarming and growing frequency. Depending on Ken's evangelical surroundings, he might have received some widely varying advice. Consider the following possibilities.

1. Some would have come down quite hard on him, showing him from Scripture not only the sinfulness of the action he contemplated, but his wrong attitude and desire. They would insist on his repentance and confession, in the process putting him under the fear of God's punishment and the promise of church discipline if he didn't conform.

2. Others might make a strong appeal to Ken to remember the love and sacrifice of Christ, taking him back to the scene of the cross to remind him of what it cost Christ to redeem him. They would call him to surrender himself, his will and his choices completely to Christ and to rededicate himself to the Savior.

3. Still others would approach Ken with psychological insights, telling him that he was really OK and his feelings were natural enough under the circumstances. What he really needed was to understand the origin of his insecurities and why he felt he needed Shelley so much. As he learned to cope with himself better, his need for Shelley would subside.

4. In some circles Ken would be asked to seek a climactic experience of the Holy Spirit, evidenced by an obvious gift of the Spirit. Those helping him would expect him, after this experience, to have a change of desire and freedom to act on it.

There might be many combinations of these approaches in actual situations. My purpose here is not to comment favorably or unfavorably on any of the suggestions I have described. Perhaps in all of them there are elements of important biblical truths that the Lord might use to help Ken. Intangibles such as a listening ear, love and care, strong prayer support and encouragement by the Christian body might add large measures of help.

What I do want to say about these approaches is that, with all their valid insights, *as I have stated them, none of them displays a full understanding of the new covenant.* Bits and pieces may be present, but there is no comprehensive setting in which to discover the spiritual privileges that are ours under the new covenant.

Ken and Shelley's predicament gave me a marvelous opportunity to see how effective the spiritual dynamics of the new covenant can be, given persons who are basically committed to the Word of God and to the Savior. As it turned out, they did not take the route that seemed so inescapable, and both grew greatly in their practical godliness. It was a cause for much thanksgiving.

Let me explain what I am talking about and in so doing show you what is ahead in this book.

It is surprisingly important for all of us as Christians to understand that God is a covenant-making God. His covenants with human beings display his desire and design to have fellowship with us, and fellowship with God is the rock-bottom foundation of our wholeness as persons.

The new covenant centers around an important fact. Believers in Jesus Christ since Pentecost have been joined to the triumphant Christ in a real union. In the face of the severe conflicts we all face, I want you to see what this union is and what it means for your life. I want you to see what new possibilities are opened up to you in prayer. I want you to see how victory over evil is now directly at hand and can be increasingly attained. I want you to see how the new covenant reality provides a secured path for your life in the will of God and gives you the means to walk in it. I want you to know the unity with other believers that Christ has made possible.

Whatever variation of Ken and Shelley's conflict you've experienced, I want you to know that you live in a new intimacy of fellowship with the living God that can bring undreamed-of power to your aid.

Tragically, evangelicals of our day do not major in new covenant truths. As a result we have a strong tendency to drift into legalism, materialism, various forms of harmful enculturation and painful forms of separatism. These experiences leave us unhappy and unfulfilled. I want you to see these things for the pitfalls they are and to opt for the new covenant way.

In part one of this book I shall seek to lay out the change from old covenant to new covenant, and in the process show what the essential understandings of the new covenant are and how the New Testament Scriptures emerged to express and implement these truths. Part two will then demonstrate how these realities can create an elevated life in Christ in prayer, victory, guidance and unity. Part three will discuss the blocks that characteristically mar that lifestyle and suggest ways to overcome them.

As a subtheme running through the book there will be an emphasis on the Scriptures and the significant way they become God's tool for creating life, faith and powerful fellowship with God. This will particularly surface in chapters four and ten.

As you read, I pray that hope and direction for your faith will be planted in your heart by the Spirit of truth.

PART I

THE CHANGE FROM OLD TO NEW

CHAPTER 1

A COVENANT-MAKING GOD

From early childhood I heard a lot of Bible teaching about covenants. Sometimes the whole history of God and man was spread out on charts as big as the side of a barn, and prominent in each major section was a covenant. The Adamic Covenant, the Noahic Covenant—when I was little I used to laugh at the way these names sounded when *ic* was put on the end of them!—the Abrahamic Covenant, the Mosaic Covenant, and on down the line.

When I got old enough to think a bit about the idea of a covenant, I got the picture of sitting down at a conference table with God and working out a deal—what I would agree to do and what he would agree to do in a kind of mutual commitment. Then one day a Bible teacher got through to me that you don't do that with God, that being God he sets all the terms. What a disappointment! That put me right back to rules again: God makes the rules and I am supposed to obey them. So what good was it to call it covenant? Call it law and be done with it!

The chart-maker era passed for me, and it was a long time before I began to think very seriously again about covenants. Then I became a Bible teacher and preacher myself, and I couldn't escape the fact that the Bible had a lot to say about covenants. I began to be aware of some things that had never registered in the early days. Surprisingly, covenants are more important to me now than ever before.

What Covenants Are All About

When the Bible talks about covenants between God and man, it is revealing much more than simply what God expects of us. Something in the very language of these covenants reveals a startling desire of God's heart. He wants to have fellowship with his people. From Genesis to Revelation we see a God who makes covenants with his people because he intends to establish and maintain a life-sharing fellowship with them. We lose sight of this reality when we think of God simply as Lawgiver and Judge. The idea of covenantal fellowship always underlies his dealings with his people.

Often associated with covenant statements are the words, "I will be their God, and they will be my people." In fact, this is one of the ways to recognize a covenant. To Abraham God said, "I will establish my covenant as an everlasting covenant between me and you . . . to be your God and the God of your descendants after you" (Gen 17:7 NIV). We think of what God did through Moses as essentially law giving, but even this came with strong covenantal words: "I will keep my covenant with you. . . . I will put my dwelling place among you. . . . I will walk among you and be your God, and you will be my people" (Lev 26:9-13 NIV). When God made a covenant with David and his heir, he described the relationship with these words, "I will establish his throne forever. I will be his father, and he will be my son. I will never take my love away from him" (1 Chron 17:12-13 NIV).

Looking at covenants from this point of view, we see that God initiates them because he desires relationship. He wants to be known, understood and loved. He wants to interact with his image-bearers. His approach to us has never been simply the cold expectation of rectitude, but has always involved his desire to know and be known. He reaches out in love and grieves when fellowship is broken. What he seeks from us is personal interaction—mind to mind, heart to heart, will to will—based on our knowledge of him.

Abraham had that kind of relationship with God. We remember the poignant story of Abraham's intercession for his nephew Lot. When the Lord visited Abraham just before destroying Sodom and Gomorrah, we hear him musing with himself: "Shall I hide from Abraham what I am about to do?" (Gen 18:17 NIV). The righteous Judge of all the earth would always do right, and certainly was under no obligation to share his plans with his servant Abraham. But Abraham, his covenant partner was more than a servant to God. He was his *friend!* Hundreds of years later in Isaiah's time, God still spoke of Abraham as his friend: "You descendants of Abraham my friend . . . do not fear, for I am with you" (Is 41:8, 10 NIV). With his friend Abraham God shared his heart and his plans.

And so it was with Moses too: "As Moses went into the tent, the pillar of cloud would come down and stay at the entrance, while the LORD spoke with Moses. . . . The LORD would speak to Moses face to face, as a man speaks with his friend" (Ex 33:9, 11 NIV).

It is our highest glory and joy to know and love God, and this he deeply wants. "And what does the LORD require of you? To act justly and to love mercy and to walk humbly with your God" (Mic 6:8 NIV). This is the heart of the idea of covenant. In discussing the Hebrew word for covenant, Gottfried Quell has said, "The concept is understood as the firmly regulated form of a fellowship between God and man."

The Covenant of Works

When Quell uses the words "firmly regulated" in connection with covenants, we get the impression that covenants are not wishy-washy expressions of sentiment. And indeed they are not! It is after all reasonable to assume that interaction between an infinitely holy, powerful, just and wise Creator, who is also loving and seeking, and a finite creature who was designed for God's glory, will have to be firmly regulated.

"Covenant of works" is one of the ways we express this demand. While not used in Scripture, this expression serves a necessary purpose in describing the God-man relationship. Not only were we created in the image of God so as to be able to interact with him, but *as creatures* we were designed to glorify and serve him. Submission to God, the fulfilling of his will, was built into our humanness. The firm regulation of fellowship, as expressed in any covenant between God and man, must include this element.

This was immediately apparent in the original state. The test of the forbidden fruit was a constant reminder to Adam and Eve that continuation of their good fellowship with God depended on continued submission. This was more than just an arbitrary law. Hosea 6:6-7 makes it plain that it was actually a covenant, "Like Adam," the passage says, "they have broken the covenant" (NIV). It was actually a covenant of works: "Do my will and live; disobey and die." Life and death meant spiritual life and spiritual death; that is, Adam and Eve would either continue to share the life of God or be alienated from his fellowship. This was a covenant that required righteous performance in order to maintain the relationship.

The requirements of the covenant of works have never been rescinded for mankind. They do not so much characterize a period of time in human history as they grow out of what it means for God to be God and for us to be human. Even our Lord Jesus, when he became human, found it necessary to "learn obedience": "And being found in appearance as a man, he humbled himself and became obedient" (Phil 2:8 NIV). For Jesus to be genuinely human, and then to represent the human race, he had to come under the covenant of works. We shall presently see that a great deal hinged on his perfect performance under that covenant.

In the final scene of judgment before the throne of God, we still find the unabated force of the covenant of works: "The dead were judged out of those things which were written in the books, according to their works. . . . They were judged every man according to their works" (Rev 20:12-13 KJV). Failure to keep that covenant results in final separation from the life of God. But thank God, there is more to be said about covenant!

The Covenant of Grace

The human race fell! Their loss of spiritual life and fellowship with God was immediately observable. From the instruction of later portions of the Bible, we know that the spiritual death that came on us made it impossible for us, indeed distasteful to us, to achieve the perfect obedience that the covenant of works required. Though the full revelation of this came gradually, God of course knew it at once. In the light of the deep-rooted rebellion and estrangement which took over human life, what a marvel to discover that God continued to love and desire fellowship with his creatures, and that there was already in his mind another covenant by which to regulate fellowship with himself. Although it was impossible to do away with the covenant of works, the alternate covenant would involve such necessary characteristics as forgiveness, mercy, grace and restoration.

This covenant, too, was deeply founded in the very nature of God. Love, mercy and forgiveness are just as truly attributes of God as his justice and holiness. Even as the one set of attributes required the covenant of works, the other required a covenant of grace to regulate sinful humanity's approach to God.

Its existence was immediately apparent in the way God dealt with his rebel creatures. He sought them, spoke to them, covered them, promised them an ultimate reversal of the calamity which Satan had engineered. Not much was known about it at the beginning, but it was obviously a covenant of grace that was designed to overcome the sad consequences of the fall and make possible a renewal of fellowship with God.

The covenant of grace, though functioning from the beginning, began to be explicitly revealed through God's dealings with Abraham. The essential feature of this covenant was faith rather than works. Abraham believed God and it was counted to him for righteousness (Gen 15:6). This covenant says "Believe and live; disbelieve and die."

In the New Testament, Paul pointed out that the initiating of the Mosaic period of law did not cut off the covenant of grace made with Abraham: "What I mean is this: the law, introduced 430 years later, does not set aside the covenant previously established by God and thus do away with the promise. . . . God in his grace gave it to Abraham through a promise" (Gal 3:17-18 NIV).

These two basic covenantal dealings of God with human beings intersect in the person and work of Jesus Christ. He kept the covenant of works perfectly for his people, paid for their failures under that covenant and established the foundations for the covenant of grace.

The covenant of grace, centering in the atoning work of Jesus Christ, is given an eternal status in Scripture. The writer of Hebrews speaks about "the blood of the eternal covenant" (Heb 13:20 NIV), and John refers to the "Lamb that was slain from the creation of the world" (Rev 13:8 NIV). At every point in human history the decrees of God are all known to him. While he works with us genuinely in our time frame, he himself is not subject to it in the same sense that we are. So at all times in the course of our fallen condition, even from the very beginning, the atonement of his Son has been a fact in God's mind. The tension between his mercy and his justice has always found its resolution here. The covenant of grace could find expression in his approach to Adam and Eve even then on the basis of Calvary. The meaning of animal sacrifices throughout Old Testament times is grounded in the picture that they gave of Christ's ultimate sacrifice, which was the real source of the forgiveness offered.

After the Fall, salvation has always been "by grace through faith" and has always been based on the saving work of Christ. Before the historical event took place outside Jerusalem, faith looked forward in some way to that event. How clear the human sight of it was is not so important as the reality of its presence in the mind of God. Even so, the growth of prophecy through the Old Testament gave increasing substance to the expectation of Messiah's work. As Paul said to Timothy, the Old Testament Scriptures "are able to make you wise for salvation through faith in Christ Jesus" (2 Tim 3:15 NIV). Since Calvary, of course, our faith looks back with increased clarity to that basis for our hope.

Thus the overall sweep of Scriptures makes it plain that both the covenant of works and the covenant of grace existed side by side throughout God's dealings with the human race. The covenant of works formed a necessary accompaniment to our creation, and the covenant of grace appeared immediately when the Fall made it necessary.

What this all says to you and me is how very much the living God desires relationship with his creatures. Our God is a covenant-maker, and all Scripture is covenant revelation, showing how God establishes fellowship with his people through the ages. If we try to take the things he offers to us in redemption without seeking to know and love him, we have missed the point of it all! We have left his desire unsatisfied.

CHAPTER 2

LIFE UNDER
THE OLD

I *was a Christian for several years before I ever read the Old Testament* through, and even then I felt that I should get some kind of medal for doing it. I was eager to be "a New Testament Christian," I think, although I didn't have a very clear idea of what I meant by that. At any rate, in my first attempts at the Old Testament, I didn't find much to excite me. Some of the stories were interesting, but I had grown up on Bible story books and then had gone through many reruns in Sunday school, so that most of these were rather worn out. I got some sort of excitement out of being able to find Zephaniah in "sword drills" quicker than others, but the "begats" and the peace offerings, the knops and taches, the kings and the wars, the Psalms of Asaph and the Selahs, and a host of other things were meaningless to me.

How sad! Today I can hardly count the ways that the Lord has blessed and directed me through the beauties of the Old Testament. I have found healing for deep hurts, conviction of sin and guidance for my life in the most surprising places. You can hardly understand the message of this book without taking a look at the old covenant.

Several Scriptures make it clear that "old covenant" refers especially to the Mosaic period of Old Testament times, rather than to the whole of the Old Testament history. The distinction between the old and new begins to appear in the major prophets. For example, here is Jeremiah's way of stating it: "I will make a new covenant with the house of Israel and with the house of Judah. It will not be like the covenant I made with their forefathers when I took them by the hand to lead them out of Egypt" (Jer 31:31-32 NIV). The old covenant is the Mosaic covenant; the new covenant is in some special sense a Messianic covenant. Both Paul and the writer of Hebrews in the New Testament associate the old covenant with Mount Sinai and thus with Moses (See Gal 4:24-26, 31 and Heb 12:18-24). In Scripture, then, "old covenant" is definitely associated with the period dominated by Mosaic law, and the "new covenant" with the period inaugurated by Christ and his work. I think it would be accurate to describe the old covenant as good, hard, and on tiptoes!

Good

The very expressions "old" and "new" and the way Scripture talks about these covenants implies an improved status under the new covenant. That improvement is what this book is all about. But don't underestimate the level of blessing that could be enjoyed by believers in the Mosaic era. It was after all a *covenant* time, and this meant something about fellowship with God, the same God we know today. Look at their faith and life for a moment.

Consider, for example, their relationship to Scripture. These believers—and this we surely must call them—frequently show a solid relationship to God's Word. They are sometimes described as those who "trembled" at God's word (see Ezra 9:4 and Is 66:2). They knew that it was the product of the Spirit of the Lord (2 Sam 23:2). They knew the need for divine illumination of their minds: "Open my eyes that I may see wonderful things in your law" (Ps 119:18 NIV). They were aware of its sanctifying impact and that it enabled a real relationship with God: "I seek you with all my heart; do not let me stray from your commands. I have hidden your word in my heart that I might not sin against you" (Ps 119:10-11 NIV).

We cannot read David's penitential Psalm (51) without realizing how strongly Old Testament believers could experience conviction of sin, repentance and forgiveness. There was a real emphasis on the inwardness and genuineness of their faith: "Trust in the LORD with all your heart," was Solomon's instruction (Prov 3:5 NIV), even as Moses himself long before had called on Israel to circumcise their hearts (Deut 10:6).

Most striking is the sense of the reality and beauty of God, the sense of praise and worship which was expressed by old covenant believers. Listen to David, for example: "One thing I ask of the LORD, this is what I seek: that I may dwell in the house of the LORD all the days of my life, to gaze upon the beauty of the LORD and to seek him in his temple" (Ps 27:4 NIV). These are the words of one whose heart was awakened to God, who valued the reality of God and wanted to "walk humbly with" him.

David's prayer shows also his awareness of the presence of God's spirit in his life: "Do not cast me from your presence or take your Holy Spirit from me" (Ps 51:11 NIV).

These characteristics of old covenant believers demonstrate the reality of God's grace in their lives. In spite of the heritage of spiritual death and separation from God that they received along with everyone else, these were people who had been made spiritually alive. They were people of God's Word; they were people of faith; they were in touch with God's Spirit. They had rich times of worship and praise. What they wrote under God's inspiration has served all subsequent generations of God's people to enrich faith and worship and to direct fellowship with God. When the little Massachusetts boy looked down his nose at the Old Testament, it was he, not it, that was impoverished!

Hard

Atonement, sacrifices, priesthood and many other expressions of grace were familiar features of Israelite worship. But after Mount Sinai the Law overshadowed all this. Its expression came to them again and again in terms of the covenant of works: "Do this and live; disobey and die." Condemnation and death indeed became terribly real. The very day Moses brought the tablets of the Law down from the mountaintop, three thousand Israelites died because of idolatry! How interesting it is that on the Day of Pentecost three thousand Jews entered into spiritual life, responding to the gospel! (see Ex 32:15-28 and Acts 2:36-41.)

In one awesome sequence of wilderness events described in Numbers, the following things happened: fire from God consumed some Israelites on the fringe of the camp because they had complained in God's hearing (11:1-3); an unspecified number of Israelites died of a plague after complaining about the food God was supplying them (11:31-34); the ten spies who brought back a bad report from the Promised Land were struck down and died (14:37-38); a man who gathered some wood on the sabbath day was stoned to death at God's instruction (15:32); Korah, Dathan and Abiram raised an insurrection and were swallowed up, along with their families, in an earthquake (16:28-30), and the 250 community leaders who had been influenced by them were consumed by fire from the Lord (16:35). When the people rose up against Moses over this incident, a plague killed almost 15,000 of them (16:46-50). Finally the people cried out in desperation, "We perish, we are dying, we are all dying! Everyone who comes near . . . to the tabernacle of the Lord must die. Are we to perish completely?" (17:12-13 NASB). God's design for his covenant people was good. But the covenant of works was receiving a terrifying demonstration before their eyes. The Law weighed heavily on them.

Perhaps there was something especially significant about those forty years in the wilderness. This was the initiation of the Mosaic period. At the end of those years, Moses summed up the experience this way: "Be careful to follow every command I am giving you. . . . Remember how the LORD your God led you . . . these forty years, to humble you and to test you in order to know what was in your heart, whether or not you would keep his commands. . . . Know then in your heart that as a man disciplines his son, so the LORD your God disciplines you. . . . If you ever forget the LORD your

God . . . I testify against you today that you will surely be destroyed. Like the nations the LORD destroyed before you, so you will be destroyed for not obeying the LORD your God" (Deut 8:1-2, 5, 19-20 NIV). The Israelites were encouraged to look back on that severe time as the discipline and heart-searching of a loving Father, yet there was no diminishing of the absolute demands of the Law.

And so it went for another thousand years and more! Never is the perspective changed. Through Ezekiel came God's awesome words, "The soul who sins will die" (18:4 NASB), and nearly the last words in our present order of the Old Testament go right back to the Mosaic beginnings: "Remember the law of my servant Moses, the decrees and laws I gave him at Horeb for all Israel" (Mal 4:4 NIV). The final phrase of Malachi is: "Lest I come and smite the land with a curse" (Mal 4:6 NASB).

If God knew from the start that his people did not have a heart to obey his commandments, that they were unable in their innate sinfulness to keep the covenant of works, why did he put them under the Law in such fashion? If he was providing atonement and forgiveness, if Calvary was in his mind all along, why such a severe program of law and works? Why the groaning, the condemnation and the death?

Besides what we have just noted, that it was a program of chastening and heart-searching, it seems clear also that it was designed to make plain the need for an inward change of heart: "Circumcise your hearts, therefore, and do not be stiff-necked any longer" (Deut 10:16 NIV).

Since there was a covenant, and fellowship with himself was one of God's goals for his people, the need for atonement and forgiveness would certainly be heightened by the severity of the law. No doubt it was God's intention to drive his people to the tabernacle, the priesthood and the offerings, all newly inaugurated, and to establish these as central to a life with God.

Also we can see that this program called for a deep, inward exercise of faith. God had already promised a future time of fulfillment. Even in the wilderness God told them that he would "raise up for them a prophet like [Moses] from among their brothers, and he will tell them everything I command him" (Deut 18:18 NIV). They were told too of a later time when "the LORD your God will circumcise your hearts and the hearts of your descendants, so that you may love him with all your heart and with all your soul, and live" (Deut 30:6 NIV). All this seems designed to give a forward look to their faith, focusing it more and more on the promised Messiah. The more constrained they were by the Law, the more people of faith would long for the coming promise of God, and this faith *would both justify and sanctify them!*

Nevertheless, the burden and pressure were extremely heavy. It was a hard time. In contrast with the new covenant, Paul and the writer of Hebrews use harsh words to describe the old scene, words like *slavery, condemnation* and *death.* Paul did indeed say that there was a glory connected with the giving of the law through Moses, but it was a fading glory, whereas the glory of the new was a surpassing glory (2 Cor 3:7-11).

As we think of what it meant for old covenant believers to be "under the law," it is worth noting that this covenant created an impassable barrier between Jews and Gentiles. A Gentile could not be united to a Jew in God's sight except by becoming a proselyte, that is, by coming under the covenant and receiving the sign of circumcision. This helps us understand the severity of the conflict over circumcision in the apostolic church.

So the old covenant times were good for many reasons and hard for other reasons. One other characteristic we must see.

On Tiptoes

As the Old Testament times moved on, the note of Messianic expectancy became clearer and fuller. There had been hints before, but now prophets began speaking of a time when the Lord would give to his people a heart of flesh in place of their stony heart, would place his Spirit within them after cleansing and purifying them, and would cause them to keep his statutes (Ezek 36:24-28). It was obvious that these promises were associated with the coming of the Messiah, and now the prophets begin to speak of a "new covenant"

(Jer 31:31-34; Ezek 37:21-29).

How exciting a thing for the prophets to meditate on this expectation! This excitement must have been shared by the godly ones in Israel who heard their messages. There was a sense in which Old Testament believers began to stand on tiptoes, straining to see what was coming. Long afterward, Peter spoke of this expectation in these words: "Concerning this salvation, the prophets, who spoke of the grace that was to come to you, searched intently and with the greatest care, trying to find out the time and circumstances to which the Spirit of Christ in them was pointing when he predicted the sufferings of Christ and the glories that would follow. It was revealed to them that they were not serving themselves but you, when they spoke of the things that have now been told you by those who preached the gospel to you by the Holy Spirit sent from heaven. Even angels long to look into these things" (1 Pet 1:10-12 NIV). *It was the Spirit of Messiah* in them who was pointing to new glories ahead. It was not to be their experience, but they looked with longing for what was coming.

"These were all commended for their faith, yet none of them received what had been promised. God had planned something better for us so that only together with us would they be made perfect" (Heb 11:39-40 NIV).

The old covenant emphasized the "land of promise" with associated material blessings. The ideal seemed to be every man under his own vine and fig tree, on his own ancestral land, blessed with the early and the latter rain, and prosperity as reward for faithful obedience to the covenant. Yet old covenant people of faith were noted for their anticipation of "the city with foundations, whose architect and builder is God. . . . They were longing for a better country— a heavenly one. . . . They admitted that they were aliens and strangers on earth" (Heb 11:10, 16, 13 NIV).

No matter how great the experience of salvation was for the old covenant believer, it was clear to the more perceptive of them that something more glorious was ahead, something so much more glorious that God himself would describe it as a new covenant in contrast with the Mosaic covenant. It was not new in the sense that it would be a covenant of grace never before in operation. Yet the Spirit of Messiah was actively bearing witness to the marvel of a coming change. Believers of old faced it with keen anticipation, even though its glory would not be part of their own experience during their earthly lives.

Jesus bore testimony to this fact when he said to his disciples: "Happy are your eyes because they see, and your ears because they hear! Many prophets and saints, I tell you, desired to see what you now see, yet never saw it; to hear what you hear, yet never heard it" (Mt 13:16-17 NEB).

So old covenant believers waited on tiptoes in the wings and watched to see the new act that would take place on the stage of redemption. And that very faith-watch was their salvation, too. It was the *old* time, but even they themselves were aware that new glory was coming, and that it would be associated with the advent of the Messiah.

CHAPTER 3

CHRIST THE TURNING POINT

Great change-over times often arrive unexpectedly. At first glance we might well wonder both at the person chosen to accomplish the turning from old to new covenants and the way he went about it. A second look, however, convinces us that he really was the only one for the task and that he did his work to perfection. While honoring and fulfilling the old, he transformed it into something glorious and new.

His name is Messiah: born in Bethlehem, the city of David, raised in Nazareth of Galilee, common class but Son of God. Angels sang at his birth, wise men came from the East, but there was little else to indicate that the turning point of the ages and of the history of mankind had come. Around 1995 we will mark anniversary year 2000 of his birth. That I have written this book and you are reading it shows that we are still trying to understand him better and what his coming meant.

For the purposes of our study, we are particularly interested to see how the coming of Jesus related to the covenants. Since our God

is ever seeking to establish fellowship with himself through covenants, and since Jesus again and again claimed for himself a pivotal
agency in establishing such fellowship, he must be centrally connected with covenants. We have also seen that the Old Testament
prophecies about a coming new covenant were connected with the
Messiah, so we are compelled to examine his life here as in some
sense a turning point in covenant history.

The Covenant Keeper

On many occasions Jesus seemed to delight in using the name "son
of man" for himself. I suppose that any person might legitimately
choose that name for himself and simply mean by it "I'm human."
But there was something about the way Jesus used it that lifted it
far beyond that common claim. Hear him say, for example, "the Son
of Man has authority on earth to forgive sins" (Mt 9:6 NIV). Or
again, "The Son of Man is Lord of the Sabbath" (Mt 12:8). And
again, "So the Son of Man will be three days and three nights in
the heart of the earth" (Mt 12:40 NIV). Another startling example
was this: "The Son of Man will send out his angels, and they will
weed out of his kingdom everything that causes sin and all who do
evil" (Mt 13:41 NIV). Although with Jesus this name must include
a claim of humanity, it is no common claim. Rather it is associated
with authority, with kingdom and with power, even power over sin
and death.

This use of the name *son of man* seems to be a claim by Jesus of
a unique identity. Probably his Jewish hearers were startled by it,
because some of them would immediately remember the passage in
Daniel where this name occurred: "I looked, and there before me
was one like a son of man, coming with the clouds of heaven. He
approached the Ancient of Days and was led into his presence. He
was given authority, glory, and sovereign power; all peoples, nations and men of every language worshiped him. His dominion is
an everlasting dominion that will not pass away, and his kingdom
is one that will never be destroyed" (Dan 7:13-14 NIV).

The way Jesus uses the name *son of man* seems nothing less than
a claim of Messiahship, but with a special emphasis on his human-

ity. He said on several occasions that "the Son of Man must be lifted up," referring to his death (see Jn 3:14; 8:28), and also "But I, when I am lifted up from the earth, will draw all men to myself" (Jn 12:32 NIV, note also 12:33-34). He appears to be claiming a unique relationship to the rest of humanity, as though representing them or acting for them in his own humanity.

After there had been time for enlargement and sharpening of concepts about Christ, it became clear that he had indeed been given a very special relationship to the people he came to save. He is sometimes called the "second" or "last Adam" (1 Cor 15:45-47; see also Rom 5:14-17). By this teaching we understand that it was given to two men to act for the human race. Adam in his disobedience acted for the race yet unborn. He received in his person a judgment which affected the entire human race. To Christ, the second and last Adam, was given once more the same capacity.

The importance of this teaching is profound. We see Jesus as the battleground where all the human problem was centered and solved. We see the person of Jesus as the place where all the results of his victory were received and where they exist in perfection. We see the Son of Man operating in behalf of all that he stood for, our representative covenant-keeper.

Now notice the importance that Jesus attached to his own obedience to the Father. Again and again he refers to it: "I tell you the truth, the Son can do nothing by himself; he can only do what he sees his Father doing. . . . By myself I can do nothing; I judge only as I hear, and my judgment is just, for I seek not to please myself but him who sent me. . . . My teaching is not my own. It comes from him who sent me. . . . I do nothing on my own but speak just what the Father has taught me. . . . The one who sent me is with me; he has not left me alone, for I always do what pleases him. . . . The Father who sent me commanded me what to say and how to say it. . . . Whatever I say is just what the Father has told me to say" (Jn 5:19, 30; 7:16; 8:28-29; 12:49-50 NIV).

Of course the second Person of the Trinity would act in harmony with the first Person! But that is not primarily what is in view here. Philippians 2:7 and 8 tells us that he took "the very nature of a servant, being made in human likeness. And being found in appearance as a man, he humbled himself and became *obedient* to death" (NIV). And Hebrews tells us that "he learned obedience" (5:8). It was not his own need that impelled him to obey his Father. It was as the Son of *Man* that he obeyed. He was acting for us; he had become our covenant-keeper, one human being operating in behalf of all he represented.

The covenant of works was upon him, as it is on all of us, but he fulfilled it perfectly in a life of total harmony with the will of his Father. This was done for us by the one who stood in our place. The righteousness of the law was his attainment, achieved by works that were faultlessly in accord with his Father's decrees. He alone of all human beings can claim from the Father the fulfillment of God's side of the covenant—spiritual life earned by good works.

There is one striking difference in Jesus' representative role as covenant-keeper. When Adam occupied this capacity, all the race was innocent and almost totally unborn. But behind Jesus lay many generations who had been promised the benefit of what he would do, and ahead were many more generations cut from the same piece of spoiled cloth. He must deal with the spoilage of the old, as well as create the new, so his path of obedience led him to a cross. There took place what provided the eternal basis for the covenant of grace. He himself said that "the Son of Man did not come to be served, but to serve, and to give his life as a ransom for many" (Mt 20:28 NIV). This was in keeping with many old covenant predictions, such as Isaiah's bittersweet description of the suffering servant, "We all, like sheep, have gone astray, each of us has turned to his own way; and the LORD has laid on him the iniquity of us all" (Is 53:6 NIV).

After Christ's earthly stay, when his followers had been helped to see more clearly what had happened at the cross, they came to realize that there God made Jesus, as though he were the only man, "to be sin for us" (2 Cor 5:21 NIV). Upon him was placed all the failure of mankind in all ages to keep the covenant of works. It is as though Jesus became *the* sinner, the *only* sinner, the sinner of all the ages! There he received the full curse of the broken covenant—both physical and spiritual death. There was wrenched from his lips the most heart-rending cry of all time, as the Son was torn away from fellowship with the Father, "My God, my God, why have you forsaken me?" We are deeply moved by this, for this is the cry of lost humanity, alienated from the life of God.

God not only made Jesus to be sin for us, but Jesus "put away sin by the sacrifice of Himself" (Heb 9:26 NASB). He became totally freed from humanity's sin that he bore. Jesus also identified himself with us so that he "might taste death for everyone" (Heb 2:9 NASB), and he "abolished death" so that "death no longer is master over Him" (2 Tim 1:10; Rom 6:9 NASB). Calvary was the hour for Satanic darkness to prevail (Lk 22:53), but this tragic dilemma of our race was resolved there also, as Christ "discarded the cosmic powers and authorities like a garment" (Col 2:15 NEB) at the cross. He is the one man alive on the other side of the grave, possessing a new resurrection body, new life, freedom from all our ills. Salvation is indeed *in Christ*, and our relationship to a covenant-making God is totally focused through our great covenant-keeper.

As we have indicated, many of these truths about the Messiah and his work were present in some degree in the Old Testament prophecies. Certainly the ideas of atonement, death, resurrection and forgiveness were there. But already, when we come to such dimensions as the full identification of Christ with those he came to save, his role as *the* covenant-keeper, *the* man, we are verging on new understandings.

The Bridge from Old to New

Jesus' person and works were central to all the expectations and covenants of the old times and central to all that the future would hold. He would be the bridge connecting both banks of time. In examining the things he said to his disciples, we see that he was constantly building that bridge in their minds so as to tie the old with what was ahead.

He gave much attention to developing their faith in him as the Messiah. At a crucial time, he took them away to a private place and tested them to see how far they had come. He was particularly interested to see what they thought of him, who they considered him to be. Peter answered for all of them, "You are the Christ [Messiah], the Son of the living God." Jesus approved this faith, saying that it had come to them from the Father.

Now satisfied that they genuinely held him as their long-awaited Messiah, Jesus began to deal with a blind spot in their understanding of what the Messiah was to do. He immediately began to teach them that the Messiah must suffer, die and rise again (see Mt 16:21). This was no part of their concept of the Messiah, and they resisted this idea right up to the day he was crucified and then raised from the dead.

On one of his appearances to them after the resurrection, Jesus reminded his disciples of his former attempts to instruct them. He said, "This is what I told you while I was still with you: Everything must be fulfilled that is written about me in the Law of Moses, the Prophets and the Psalms." The text of Luke goes on to say, "Then he opened their minds so that they could understand the Scriptures. He told them, 'This is what is written: The Christ will suffer and rise from the dead on the third day, and repentance and forgiveness of sins will be preached in his name to all nations, beginning at Jerusalem. You are witnesses of these things' " (Lk 24:44-47 NIV).

This unique Bible study made a permanent impression on the disciples. They now understood that the good news centered in the death and resurrection of the Messiah and that it had its roots solidly in the Old Testament. It became their message mandate for all the days ahead, and the book of Acts clearly records their faithfulness in telling it. On Pentecost we hear Peter quoting from David's writings regarding the resurrection, a clear reflection of Jesus' lesson. Repeatedly the apostles spoke of the death and resurrection of Christ, of repentance and forgiveness. They identified Jesus as the Messiah.

This became true of those who came on the scene after the original disciples. Paul, though not in the group that heard Jesus give this mandate, somehow received it and committed himself to it. In Thessalonica, "as his custom was, Paul went into the synagogue, and on three Sabbath days he reasoned with them from the Scriptures, explaining and proving that the Christ had to suffer and rise from the dead. 'This Jesus I am proclaiming to you is the Christ [Messiah],' he said" (Acts 17:2-3 NIV). Much later on Paul said to King Agrippa II, "having obtained help from God, I stand to this day testifying both to small and great, stating nothing but what the Prophets and Moses said was going to take place; that the Christ was to suffer, and that by reason of His resurrection from the dead He should be the first to proclaim light both to the Jewish people and to the Gentiles" (Acts 26:22-23 NASB).

In the final period of his ministry, Paul rejoices over Timothy with these words (among the last he wrote), "From infancy you have known the holy Scriptures, which are able to make you wise for salvation through faith in Christ Jesus" (2 Tim 3:15 NIV). And here again, especially since he refers to Timothy's life from childhood, this has to be a reference to Old Testament Scriptures. The essential elements of the gospel were there. They became the mandated message of the new church after Jesus explained them to his disciples. It was quite possible to preach the gospel of Christ from the Old Testament, and the apostles did it consistently before there were any New Testament Scriptures. This, of course, fits a special emphasis Christ made; namely, that he had not come to destroy the Law or the Prophets but to fulfill them (see Mt. 5:17). So again Christ was the bridge from old to new.

The Initiator of New Understandings

People who heard Jesus teach were repeatedly struck by his fresh and authoritative manner. He did not teach like the scribes of his day, who simply repeated previous authorities. In fact, he dared to preface some of his remarks like this: "You have heard that it was said . . . but I tell you" (Mt 5:21, 27 NIV). Sometimes he cut deeply against the grain of their enculturated ideas. For example, he said, "You have heard that it was said, 'Love your neighbor and hate your enemy.' But I tell you, 'Love your enemies and pray for those who persecute you' " (Mt 5:43-44 NIV). Here his words must have jarred his hearers to the core. Under the Law they had become enculturated with strong feelings of punishment and retribution, attitudes which they felt were legitimate to express toward their enemies.

Jesus must have sounded preposterously bold in placing such startling new understandings before them. This was similarly true when he taught about the sabbath and on many other subjects.

More than this, Jesus actually began to imply that a new era of revelation was being initiated with his presence and teaching. In Matthew 13, answering the disciples' question as to why he was speaking to the crowd in parables, he said, "To you it has been granted to know the mysteries of the kingdom of heaven, but to them it has not been granted." And then a moment later, "Many prophets and righteous men desired to see what you see, but did not see it; and to hear what you hear, and did not hear it" (Mt 13:11, 17 NASB). He seems to be indicating that a new and distinctive stage of revelation was emerging. In fact, at the end of this discussion, he said, "Every teacher of the law who has been instructed about the kingdom of heaven is like the owner of a house who brings out of his storeroom *new* treasures as well as *old*" (Mt 13:52 NIV, italics added).

Not only did Jesus explain what the prophets had said about the Messiah's atoning death and resurrection, thus bridging the past and the future, but he also began teaching things that had a new sound altogether. They particularly had to do with their relationship to his person. He talked about the necessity of their eating his flesh and drinking his blood (Jn 6:53). He talked about his being the vine and their being the branches (Jn 15:5). He taught them that he was going back to the Father to receive his glory and to provide them with a new relationship with the Holy Spirit. He taught them in considerable detail about this Comforter who was to come and what his presence would mean to them (Jn 14—17). A climax of these daring innovations came when Jesus placed new significance on the Passover observance, transforming it into the Christian communion service, and using for the first and only time the expression "new covenant": "This cup is the new covenant in my blood" (1 Cor 11:25 NIV).

There was little, if anything, in the Old Testament to prepare those who were about him for the scope of these new understandings. They probably did not grasp much of it at the time, nevertheless it was the beginning of new covenant revelation.

In the midst of these new teachings at the very end of his time with the disciples, Jesus made a specific prediction of great importance. He told his disciples to expect additional teaching from him after the completion of his earthly ministry: "I have many more things to say to you," he said, "but you cannot bear them now. But when He, the Spirit of truth comes, He will guide you into all the truth; for He will not speak on His own initiative, but whatever He hears, He will speak; and He will disclose to you what is to come" (Jn 16:12-13 NASB). While Christians have always rightly taken this promise to be an assurance of the general teaching ministry of the Holy Spirit, one of its direct and immediate references was to special apostolic instruction which they would later receive.

Jesus ascended out of his disciples' sight. Their understanding of the experiences they had just been through was only fragmentary. But some things they knew: that Jesus of Nazareth was their Messiah, they had no doubt; that he had died in a most unusual way and with much significance, they knew; that the earth had broken open and one Man was alive on the other side of death, they knew. They had touched him, eaten with him, talked with him after his resurrection. Exactly where he had gone and what he was now doing they probably couldn't have said, but they knew that more understanding had been promised, and they were waiting for a special coming of the Holy Spirit. They couldn't have described it this way, but they were stepping into the era of the new covenant, and they were feeling some of the excitement of this.

CHAPTER 4

UNVEILING THE NEW

From the time I became a Christian in the early 1930s, I was exposed to a typical form of discipling through a variety of agencies—Sunday school, Christian camps and conferences, dedicated parents, evangelical literature, a Christian college (Wheaton), and much preaching and teaching. Written large in all the instruction for Christian growth was the axiom "Thou shalt have thy Quiet Time." I was told dozens of times, "If you do not read your Bible daily, you will not get your spiritual food, and you will dry up spiritually."

When I myself became a communicator of the gospel, I passed on the same advice to many Christians. Both for myself and through me to others, I'm sure it sounded like the eleventh commandment. One result for me was that the practice of daily devotional attention to the Scriptures became one of my highest priorities in life, and I have much cause to be thankful for that.

Something, however, was missing in my understanding of what I was doing. Though I frequently met God and was deeply blessed in these times, my motive for having them was often and chiefly that I must, that I needed them for my own good. For many years I had little awareness that a covenant-making God wanted to be loved and known, wanted to be sought and understood, wanted fellowship with me! I did not fully realize that Scripture was his self-revelation, his instrument for creating and maintaining that fellowship with him, even as it creates life and faith. It still astounds me to think that a major motive for my devotional use of the Bible is to please him—to satisfy his desire to interact with me, his desire to be loved by me. I knew the Bible was important, but I didn't really understand all of the reasons.

At the very beginning of the Mosaic covenant, God started the process of giving a written word to accompany it. To the tables of stone written with God's finger were added the writings of Moses, and then the collections of historical, poetical and prophetical writings that rounded out the Old Testament. It would have been impossible for God's people of that era to enter into covenant fellowship with God without those Scriptures.

Meredith Kline says, "Canon [Scripture] is inherent in covenant." If covenant is God's way of establishing and maintaining fellowship with himself, then the accompanying Scriptures must play an instrumental role in that process.

This involves more than simply imparting information to our minds. In his hands God's Word has creative power, that is, power to bring into reality what God describes in it. When we look carefully at the way God used the prophets, we realize that he was not simply describing things that would happen, but was using his mouthpieces to *cause* them to happen. So he tells Jeremiah, "Now, I have put my words in your mouth. See, today I appoint you over nations and kingdoms to uproot and tear down, to destroy and overthrow, to build and to plant" (Jer 1:9-10 NIV). Did Jeremiah destroy and build nations with physical instruments of war and peace? No, indeed! He did it by uttering God's Word, which had the power to tear down and to create (see Hos 6:6).

God designed the new covenant era to produce a "surpassing glory" of fellowship and made new revelations of himself to bring it about. After a gap of at least 400 years from the last scriptures of the old covenant era, this is exactly what happened. The writer of Hebrews tells us that God spoke in the old era "by the prophets," but in the present era "by a Son" (Heb 1:1-3). In some unique way the new covenant revelations were spoken by Jesus Christ. They were not merely a restatement of the Old Testament, but they contained the essential understandings of the new covenant fellowship. They became the instrument in God's hands for powerful creation of what they described.

In this chapter we are watching the fascinating process by which new covenant revelations started our era, realizing that this is what opened the door for our own elevation of fellowship with God.

A Little Jew from Tarsus

The original disciples were not the first to receive the new covenant revelations from the risen Christ. The story rather began to unfold through a little Jew from Tarsus. His given name was Saul, but later he became better known as Paul. Intense, intellectual, operating with persistent zeal, this well-educated Pharisee became the first mouthpiece for Jesus' new covenant word.

Paul's Christian experience began with a shattering confrontation between him and the exalted Christ. Imagine the drama of the situation. Paul had stood by the dying Stephen a couple of years before and had heard him claim to look into heaven and see the Son of Man standing at the right hand of God. Paul had been enraged at what seemed to him the height of blasphemy. Now, outside Damascus he himself is struck down by the flashing brilliance of heaven and hears the voice asking, "Saul, Saul, why do you persecute me?" Clutched by fear Paul asks, *"Who are you, Lord?"* Then the royal voice replies, "I am Jesus," and Paul's whole early life comes crashing down around him. Christ's foe becomes his slave (see Acts 9:1-9).

This was only the beginning of such direct confrontations with Christ. Three years later Paul escaped from Damascus and went to Jerusalem. After only two weeks of tension-filled ministry, Jesus appeared to Paul in the temple and told him to leave Jerusalem (Acts 22:17-21). Other direct appearances are recorded in Acts 18:9 and

23:11. How *real* the living Christ must have been to Paul! Paul apparently felt that these appearances tied him in with the other disciples who had seen the risen Lord. They validated his apostleship. In writing to the Corinthians about the resurrection appearances, he added himself to the list: "And last of all, as it were to one untimely born, He appeared to me also" (1 Cor 15:8 NASB).

In addition to these direct appearances, Paul spoke of having much communication from the Lord in the form of revelations. He strongly affirmed to the Galatian believers that his gospel was shaped by such direct revelations: "I want you to know, brothers, that the gospel I preached is not something that man made up. I did not receive it from any man, nor was I taught it; rather, I received it by revelation from Jesus Christ" (Gal 1:11-12 NIV). He implies that his trip into the desert of Arabia involved some of this direct establishment of the content of his message. Indeed, the whole tenor of his argument in this portion of Galatians is that for the first fourteen years of his Christian life he had no opportunity to discuss his message with other leaders of the church. I find it astounding to hear him introduce his account of the Last Supper with these words, *"For I received from the Lord* what I also passed on to you: The Lord Jesus, on the night he was betrayed, took bread" (1 Cor 11:23 NIV, italics added). Even his knowledge of the events and sayings of Christ's earthly ministry were apparently a direct gift from Christ.

After the Jerusalem leaders (and the Lord) sent Paul home to Tarsus (Acts 9:26-30), he drops out of the Acts account completely until Barnabas enlists his help for the booming new witness at Antioch. During this silent period of five or six years, various indications point to his preaching (Gal 1:21-23), establishing churches (the letter from the Jerusalem council in Acts 15 was addressed to the churches in Syria and Cilicia, the area around Tarsus), and suffering severe persecutions (many of those listed in 2 Corinthians 11 must fit in this period).

During the silent years Paul apparently received more direct revelations from the Lord. In 2 Corinthians 12, in a roundabout way Paul tells of receiving "surpassingly great revelations" from the

Lord, and also a physical infirmity that was designed to keep him humble and dependent on grace, even while blessed with great revelations. Paul says that these revelations occurred fourteen years earlier, and this would place them near the end of the silent years. So the man Barnabas brought to Antioch was probably already the most knowledgeable Christian in the church—knowledgeable not just in regard to the Old Testament and the facts of Christ's earthly ministry, but with new insights that Christ had been giving him in the midst of much suffering.

Antioch was a new kind of experience for Paul. He was part of a ministering team which included Barnabas, an emissary of the Jerusalem church. Although he had now been ministering for eight or nine years, this was his first opportunity to hear other forms of teaching. You may be sure that he was an eager listener when the others spoke, and when Paul taught, it must have been an astonishing experience to his coworkers. The depth and penetration of his grasp of Christ was startling. The combined ministry was deeply fruitful that year; for the first time in history believers became known as "Christians" (Acts 11:26).

Part of the spiritual vigor at Antioch became focused in a new missionary enterprise. The Holy Spirit sent out Barnabas and Paul to preach the gospel across Cyprus, north to the mainland and into the area sometimes called South Galatia. The events of this journey, recorded in Acts 13 and 14, must have taken the best part of three years and resulted in several new churches. Even an initial organizing of these groups under elders was accomplished before the missionaries made their way back to Antioch.

They must have arrived back at the home church around A.D. 48. By now Paul was probably in his midforties; he had been a servant of Christ for about thirteen years; he had had much opportunity to mature personally and to develop his message around the new understandings he had received. He was about to go through two years or so of great crisis. Neither he nor the church of Christ would be the same again.

Judging from Paul's prayer life (as found in his letters) and from his concern to support the development of his converts (see 2 Cor

11:28-29), we can assume that Paul and Barnabas must have prayed earnestly and daily for the new believers in Galatia.

Before long Paul was strongly moved—indeed he says it was by revelation—to make a trip to Jerusalem (Gal 2:1-2). He was convinced that Christ himself had given him the message that he preached; he had had much opportunity to develop it and use it, along with the insights of others, in the Antioch ministry and on the mission field. He had seen its effect and the Lord's blessing on it. But he had never talked with the leaders at the mother church in Jerusalem about it. Now it was time to compare notes with them. Barnabas went with him, and they took along Titus, a Gentile, apparently one of Paul's converts (see Tit 1:4).

In Jerusalem Paul and Barnabas met with Peter, James and John, three "pillars" of the church. What a session they must have had! For the first time the Jerusalem leaders heard Paul's account of how the Lord Jesus had repeatedly appeared to him and had been giving him direct revelations regarding the gospel. He told them of his experiences in Arabia and the astonishing revelations during the years of ministry around Tarsus. They heard of events at Antioch, Cyprus and Galatia. They shared their own perspectives on the Lord's work in Jerusalem. And when they had finished talking and praying about it, *they gave to Paul and Barnabas the right hand of fellowship* and said, "we have nothing to add to your gospel!" (Gal 2:6).

It is startling to imagine these men seriously discussing their common message of Christ. The Jerusalem leaders must have thought long and hard about the new insights being eloquently put forward by Paul and his claim that Jesus was giving them to him. Perhaps they prayed earnestly together. Their unity is really astonishing. And here in Paul, Peter, James and John sat the men who would write twenty-one of the twenty-seven New Testament books!

A Question of Circumcision

Not all was joy on this trip, however. While there, Titus became the center of a severe argument. Paul felt so strongly about it afterward that he used these words to describe people who had tried to force

Titus to be circumcised: "Some false brothers had infiltrated our ranks to spy on the freedom we have in Christ Jesus and to make us slaves. We did not give in to them for a moment, so that the truth of the gospel might remain with you" (Gal 2:4-5 NIV). You may be sure that Paul went back to Antioch with a bad taste in his mouth over this incident.

Perhaps Paul and Barnabas urged the Jerusalem leaders to visit the Antioch church. Or perhaps the discussion opened up such a startling picture of the Jew/Gentile mixture of believers in that church that the Jerusalem leaders decided to get a firsthand view of it. At any rate, it was not long before Peter arrived in Antioch for a visit. A bit later a delegation from James arrived.

While Peter was in Antioch by himself, he found it quite comfortable to mingle with the Gentiles and enjoy the free fellowship that marked this church. But the delegation from James was at least partly made up of "the circumcision party" (Gal 2:12), and their strong protests swayed Peter, and eventually Barnabas and the Jewish believers in Antioch, to separate from the Gentiles. It was a grievous situation to Paul, and he reacted strongly. His public rebuke of Peter set forth in basic terms the truth of justification by faith and hopefully brought about a restoration of peace. It was obvious, however, that very sincere and earnest people were on both sides of this issue. Unless something was done soon about this difference of opinion, it might well split the church everywhere.

The next turn of events must have greatly strengthened this conviction. Whether or not the "circumcision party" that had come from Jerusalem to Antioch felt it necessary to travel on another 125 miles to visit the churches in South Galatia, we do not know. At any rate, word soon came to Antioch that pressure from the circumcision party had been brought to bear on the new Christians in Galatia, and that the believers there were not grounded solidly enough to withstand it. In the light of the previous disturbance at Antioch, this was understandable. But it was catastrophic news to Paul. He had not been there to protest. His precious new brothers and sisters in Christ were slipping away from the purity of the gospel! It was intolerable! Something must be done, and quickly.

What was done was the immediate, fervent writing of the letter to the Galatians. In it we have an expanded version of the very things he had said in Antioch when he rebuked Peter to his face. The fact that Paul made no use of the official pronouncement of the Jerusalem Council on this subject in his letter to the Galatians makes it quite likely that he wrote before the Council met. His agony knows no relief, such as the Council decision would later give. The letter is torn from his heart at white heat, as though there were no other recourse.

But what sounds are these? After relating how he received his message directly from the Lord and later checked it out with the Jerusalem leaders, Paul talks about justification by faith. This, of course, had a strong Old Testament root. But then he speaks about being "crucified with Christ" and "dying to the Law" (2:19-20). He speaks of "receiving the Holy Spirit by the hearing of faith" (3:2). He makes this the ultimate "blessing of Abraham" (3:14) and denies that the temporary adding of the Mosaic law could alter this (3:17-24). He talks of the "fullness of time" when Jesus came to "redeem those who were under the law" (4:4-5), and says that Christians are no longer slaves but sons and have the Spirit of sonship in their hearts (4:6-7). He talks about Christ being "formed in them" (4:19 NIV). These are powerful expressions of a new kind; they are not Old Testament sounds. Indeed, in the latter part of chapter four, Paul talks about two covenants, "one proceding from Mount Sinai," the other represented as the "Jerusalem above," which is free. He calls on these Christians to forsake the circumcision idea and remain in their new Christ-given freedom.

Another new understanding comes out in chapter five. There Paul talks about the works of the flesh and the fruit of the Spirit and the internal conflict between flesh and Spirit within the believer. This conflict grows out of a new intimacy with the indwelling Spirit and is to be resolved by crucifixion with Christ and a walk in the Spirit.

This writing is on a level far beyond Old Testament conceptions, even the prophecies there about the new covenant. It is climaxed in chapter six by his grand concluding idea: "May I never boast except in the cross of our Lord Jesus Christ, through which the world has been crucified to me, and I to the world. Neither circumcision nor uncircumcision means anything; what counts is a new creation. Peace and mercy to all who follow this rule, even to the Israel of God" (Gal 6:14-16 NIV). This is a magnificent New Covenant understanding.

Galatians was written with a lot of raw energy and agony. Yet with regard to the message Paul was giving in it, we do not at all get the impression that he was feeling his way. In fact, he makes a point that it was the same message he had presented to them orally when he brought the gospel to them (1:6-9 and 3:1). Also his argument in chapter one is that this is the gospel that had been revealed to him by Christ long before. The message of Galatians was not new to Paul when he wrote it; what was new was *that it was being written.* The New Testament Scriptures were making their appearance!

I wonder if Paul made a copy of this letter. If he could write it once, he could write it twice. Or someone else could copy it for him. The praying Christians in Antioch who shared his concern for the new converts may well have desired a copy of this letter for their own study. We may conjecture that this letter became well known in Antioch, as well as in the Galatian churches. Also Paul knew that this issue was headed for a showdown and would probably want a copy of this letter for use then.

The crisis did in fact come to a head, probably quite soon, and a church council was called at Jerusalem. Once more Paul and Barnabas headed for Jerusalem, and it is probable that the letter to the Galatians went with them. From Acts 15 we know that the Council, after significant public statements from Peter, Paul and Barnabas, and James, finally resolved the issue in favor of the position Paul had articulated. Probably the Holy Spirit used many things to bring them to unity. How strategic had been the earlier revelation by the Lord that sent Paul to Jerusalem to check out his gospel! How important his public rebuke of Peter at Antioch! How noteworthy the willingness of these men to be united! And how wonderful an event it was, if Peter and James indeed had read Galatians before going into the Council sessions!

At any rate, the first portion of new covenant Scriptures now existed (for further material on the date of Galatians, see the Appendix). The timing and circumstances of its writing may well have provided a situation in which a large portion of the existing church—on the mission field, at Antioch and at Jerusalem—became almost immediately aware of it and powerfully influenced by it. Some perhaps were greatly alarmed by it, but many must have been aware of the Holy Spirit's powerful attestation of it. The action of the Jerusalem Council may actually indicate this. When James announced the decision of the Council with the words, "It seemed good to the Holy Spirit and to us," he may have been speaking not only of the united subjective witness of what the Holy Spirit wanted, but of the Holy Spirit's speaking through the Word, the first written Word of the New Testament.

The Heart of the New Revelations

In the preceding chapter we noted how Jesus began to teach truths that had a decidedly new sound to them. He also indicated that he had more to say through the Holy Spirit later. Now Paul was experiencing this direct teaching from Jesus. Just how new did he think these new ideas were? One way he speaks of them is found in what are called his "mystery" passages.

In nearly twenty passages Paul uses the word mystery. It is quickly obvious why he uses that term. Repeatedly we catch phrases like "mystery hidden for long ages past, but now revealed" (Rom 16: 25-26 NIV); "my insight into the mystery of Christ, which was not made known to men in other generations as it has now been revealed by the Spirit to God's holy apostles and prophets" (Eph 3:4-5 NIV); and "this mystery, which for ages past was kept hidden in God" (Eph 3:9 NIV). Paul is talking about new revelation, something not present in the Old Testament, but now being revealed to the apostles and prophets, most particularly to himself. These are new concepts associated with the new covenant era. Let us pinpoint from these passages the ideas that Paul considered to be new.

The most comprehensive descriptions of the nature of the mystery revelations are found in Paul's prison letters. A grand statement of the central theme occurs in Ephesians 1: "For he has made known to us . . . the mystery of his will, according to his purpose which he set forth in Christ as a plan for the fulness of time, *to unite all things in him*" (1:8-10 RSV). Here is a look at Christ far beyond any conception of the Old Testament—a drawing together in his person of all things heavenly and earthly. Paul particularizes by saying, "In him . . . *we* who first hoped in Christ have been destined and appointed to live for the praise of his glory," an apparent reference to Jewish believers. Then, "In him *you* also, who have heard the word of truth, the gospel of your salvation, and have believed in him, were sealed with the promised Holy Spirit . . . to the praise of his glory," a reference to later Gentile believers (Eph 1:11-14 RSV). This drawing together of all things in the Messiah was to involve both Jewish and Gentile believers in a spiritual union with Christ. Here is an astounding new covenant understanding!

Notice also in this passage the expression, "a plan for the fulness of time, to unite all things in him" (Eph 1:10). It wasn't just the *revelation* of the mystery that was new, but the actual union itself was a new development, created by the finished work of Christ in the fullness of time.

The Jew/Gentile union in one body is the definition of mystery elsewhere, too: in Ephesians 3:4-6, Paul speaks of the "mystery of Christ, . . . that is, how the Gentiles are fellow heirs, members of the same body, and partakers of the promise in Christ Jesus through the gospel" (RSV).

Another statement of the mystery is in Colossians: "God has chosen to make known among the Gentiles the glorious riches of this mystery, which is Christ in you, the hope of glory" (1:27 NIV). Here the indwelling presence of Christ is a powerful way of expressing union with Christ. Significant here also is the fact that God was now making this reality known among the Gentiles. They were now being indwelt by Christ, just as surely as Jewish believers were. This joint union of all believers with the living and exalted Messiah was a glorious new reality not envisioned by the Old Testament prophets.

Since the exciting new revelations centered in a new intimacy with God in Christ, brought about by the indwelling Spirit, this obviously must be *new covenant* truth. Covenant has to do with fellowship with God, so Jesus had ushered in new covenant times.

Writing the New Revelations

In 1 Corinthian 2 occurs what is chronologically the first of the "mystery" passages. In it Paul describes how he brought his message to the Corinthians at the beginning of his ministry there. Bear in mind that though he is writing this letter about A.D. 55 or 56, he is describing his preaching back in A.D. 51 at Corinth. This is only a year after the Jerusalem Council and two years after Galatians was written.

Paul tells the Corinthians that the center of his message was "Jesus Christ and him crucified" (1 Cor 2:2), and that it was given not in human wisdom, "but in demonstration of the Spirit and of power" (2:4). Nevertheless, it was wisdom, "God's wisdom in a mystery, the hidden wisdom, which God predestined before the ages to our glory" (2:7 NASB). Then he paraphrases Isaiah 64:4: "No eye has seen, no ear has heard, no mind has conceived what God has prepared for those who love him" (2:9 NIV). Here is a clear indication of the fact that in old covenant times believers knew that something was coming, but did not know what it was.

Then Paul makes his great claim: "But God has revealed it to us by his Spirit. . . . We have not received the spirit of the world but the Spirit who is from God, that we may understand what God has freely given us" (2:10, 12 NIV). Hear the astounding thing Paul says next: "This is what we speak, not in words taught by human wisdom *but in words taught by the Spirit*. . . . We have the mind of Christ" (2:13, 16 NIV). Dare we consider this a claim of verbal inspiration for Paul's new covenant message? Surely it is close to that! We distinctly get the impression that Paul, even in his oral presentations, considered himself a direct channel for new revelations from Jesus Christ and that these revelations had a definite verbal character.

This impression is strengthened by statements which occur frequently in both Corinthian letters: "This is how one should regard us . . . as servants of Christ, and stewards of the mysteries of God" (1 Cor 4:1 RSV); "For I received from the Lord what I also passed on to you" (1 Cor 11:23 NIV); "as men of sincerity, as commissioned by God, in the sight of God we speak in Christ" (2 Cor 2:17 RSV); "He has made us competent as ministers of a new covenant" (2 Cor 3:6 NIV); "as the truth of Christ is in me, this boasting of mine will not be stopped" (2 Cor 11:10 NASB); and finally, "since you are demanding proof that Christ is speaking through me" (2 Cor 13:3 NIV).

As noted earlier, Paul was strongly convinced that the basic gospel of Christ—the atonement/resurrection/forgiveness framework by which to understand the Messiah—came straight out of the Old Testament. He declared himself to be an apostle "set apart for the gospel of God—the gospel he promised beforehand through his prophets in the Holy Scriptures regarding his Son . . . declared with power to be the Son of God by his resurrection from the dead" (Rom 1:1-4 NIV). He also states that "the Law and the Prophets" testify of a "righteousness from God, apart from law" (Rom 3:21 NIV) and so revealed his perception that justification by faith also had its roots in the Old Testament prophets.

In the "mystery" passages, however, Paul talks of truths not previously revealed, of new revelations now being made by the Holy Spirit to "apostles and prophets" (Eph 3:5 NIV), particularly to himself (Eph 3:3). These are New Testament "prophets," and it is significant that Paul soon goes beyond talk of a spoken message to indicate that it was being written (Eph 3:3-4). The fact that this message is being received by New Testament prophets, that it is of the character of new revelation by the Holy Spirit and that it was truth not previously revealed compels us to believe that Paul is referring to the writing of New Testament Scriptures.

With this background it becomes possible to place a surprising interpretation on Paul's benediction at the end of Romans—another "mystery" passage. "Now to Him who is able to establish you according to my gospel and the preaching of Jesus Christ, according to the revelation of the mystery which has been kept secret for long ages past, but now is manifested, and by the Scriptures of the prophets . . . has been made known to all the nations, leading to obedience of faith; to the only wise God, through Jesus Christ, be the glory forever. Amen" (Rom 16:25-27 NASB). The question is: What prophets are these? And what Scriptures are these?

Most commentators assume that this is a reference to Old Testament prophets and Scriptures. But it has all the telltale earmarks of the "mystery" settings in which Paul claims new revelations elsewhere. Paul refers to "my gospel," which he places in tandem with "the preaching of Jesus Christ." It is also "according to the revelation of the mystery which has been kept secret for long ages past, but *now* is manifested and by the Scriptures of the prophets . . . has been made known to all nations." The force of the "now" applies grammatically to both phrases that follow it: "now it has been manifested and now it has been made known by the Scriptures of the prophets."

The commentator Godet says about this passage, "These writings are represented as the means of propagating a new revelation, and should consequently designate new prophetical writings. . . . Paul himself feels that the letter which he has just written has this character, and that it ranks among the means which God is using to carry out the publication of the new revelation. It is therefore of this very letter, as well as the other letters which had proceeded from his pen, or from that of his colleagues, that he is speaking in our passage . . . a new series of inspired writings coming to complete the collection of the ancient and well-known books."

If Paul had said "apostles and prophets" in the Romans 16 passage, as he did later in Ephesians, the identification of these Scriptures as New Testament writings would be positive. But the setting is the same in both cases, and I believe that what we have here is a powerful awareness that new Scriptures were being produced by the New Testament apostles and prophets, centering around the mystery of Christ.

Paul's own role in this was central. Near the end of his ministry he refers to God in these words: "At his appointed season he brought his word to light through the preaching entrusted to me by the command of God our Savior" (Tit 1:3 NIV).

Peter confirms this high view of Paul's writings when he says that they "contain some things that are hard to understand, which ignorant and unstable people distort, *as they do the other Scriptures*, to their own destruction" (2 Pet 3:15-16 NIV, italics added). Peter classed Paul's letters as Scripture.

Nine persons produced the New Testament. The picture that emerges is that they were known to each other, aware of each other's ideas, interacted frequently and were deeply influenced by the thoughts which first began to be expressed by Paul. They were sharply aware that Jesus Christ was speaking through them, even as he had promised to do, and that what he was saying had a definite verbal character. At a remarkably early time they became aware that the new revelations were taking the form of new Scriptures.

The new revelations centered around a new covenant understanding of Christ's great redemption. They provided a marked contrast with the old covenant, though related to it. In Christ, the covenant-making God brought all covenants to a grand culmination. And through the writing of the New Testament documents he made sure that all ages could enter into its surpassing glory. New covenant Scriptures would now become a powerful instrument in God's hands to produce a new level of fellowship with God.

CHAPTER 5

THE HEART
OF THE MATTER

We have considered some of the powerful movements of the Spirit which took place in the first-century church and left us with a new portion of the Bible, a new covenant management of fellowship with God and new possibilities for living. As we seek to draw these together and look at them in this chapter, we might do well to assess how much these distinctive characteristics of the new covenant message—at the very heart of the New Testament— are a part of our thinking and life. If we know them but find them still on the fringe of our thinking, it may be that we have some new depths to plumb in our Christian experience.

Bear in mind that salvation by grace through faith is not unique to the New Testament. The atoning death of Christ along with his resurrection are not in themselves new either. The gospel preached on the day of Pentecost in Acts 2 was preached straight out of the Old Testament. It was sufficient to produce faith in Christ. We have already considered in chapter three the magnificent truth that Jesus became the great covenant-keeper of all ages, and perhaps in this reality some strong new insights begin to be added to the old message. But the striking keynotes of new covenant thought begin with what happened to Jesus after his resurrection.

The Covenant-Keeper Glorified

Old Testament prophets knew that in the last days a new creation would replace the old (Is 65:17). What they did not know was that this new creation would begin outside the walls of Jerusalem in the resurrected body of the Messiah. They had no idea that Jesus' death and resurrection would spell both the end of the old and the beginning of the new. New Testament terminology is surprising: "When anyone is united to Christ, there is a new world [literally, "creation"]; the old order has gone, and a new order has begun." Sin is spoken of as "put away," death "abolished," Satan "destroyed," and this present world "crucified." Each of these enemies we know all too well as part of our present experience, so it is only in the person of Christ that the change can be described in such final terms. Nevertheless, the new creation *has begun!* It *does* exist! There *is* a new humanity which is perfectly righteous and holy, and where all the former enemies have been defeated. It fully exists now only in Jesus himself, but even this is marvelously significant for you and me.

Indeed, this was enough to cause Paul to say to the Galatians: "Neither circumcision nor uncircumcision means anything; what counts is a new creation" (6:15 NIV). The existence of the new creation in Christ made the former distinctions obsolete! They were not obsolete until the new creation actually came into existence, so the work of Christ drastically changed things. "He himself is our peace, who has made the two one and has destroyed the barrier . . . . His purpose was to create in himself one new man out of the two" (Eph 2:14-15 NIV). No wonder Paul agonized so much over the teachings of the circumcision party!

Just before the final events of his earthly ministry, Jesus prayed this startling prayer: "Now, Father, glorify me in your presence with the glory I had with you before the world began" (Jn 17:5 NIV). This glory of his *deity* had been veiled while Jesus was on earth; now he asks for its restoration. But in Hebrews the writer speaks of the lost glory of *humanity*, now nowhere to be seen in the rest of the human race. Then he says, "But we see Jesus, who was made a little lower than the angels [that is, was made human], now crowned with glory and honor because he suffered death" (2:9 NIV). In his present risen, exalted state, Jesus not only has received back the full glory of his deity, but has been crowned with the lost glory of humanity.

Our covenant-keeping Head has received in his own person all the glory that God planned for mankind, in addition to his divine glory. Very little of this had been known by the Old Testament prophets. At best they knew that the Spirit of Messiah in them was pointing ahead to his sufferings and to glories that would follow. It is indeed a new glory. It is Christ's present glory and a part of new covenant reality.

The Covenant-Keeper Intercedes

The writer of Hebrews says, "The point of what we are saying is this: We do have such a High Priest, who sat down at the right hand of the throne of the majesty in heaven, and who serves in the sanctuary, the true tabernacle set up by the Lord, not by man" (8:1-2 NIV). He then goes on to say that this ministry of Christ is a better ministry than that of the Levitical priests and rests on a superior covenant, the new covenant, which has made the old covenant obsolete (8:6-13). In the previous chapter, the writer calls this heavenly ministry of Christ a ministry of intercession for us: "Because Jesus lives forever, he has a permanent priesthood. . . . He always lives to intercede for them" (7:24-25 NIV). Paul makes the same kind of statement: "Christ Jesus, who died—more than that, who was raised to life—is at the right hand of God and is also interceding for us" (Rom 8:34 NIV).

Jesus has already received in his own person the full fruit of his redemptive work. He stands before the Father as the glorified Head of a new race. Now he claims that fruit for his own. He is to bring many after him into glory (Heb 2:10). He has kept the covenant requirements for us perfectly. Everything of righteousness, godliness, grace, power, victory, exaltation, kingdom, future—yes, heaven itself, he claims for his people on the basis of what he has done. The Father cannot turn away his Son! Here is the most important prayer being prayed in the universe. It is the prevailing intercession of the covenant-keeper.

And since this is covenant prayer, all the blessings being secured by it are bound up in one: living fellowship with God. One of the very first great exercises of his covenant intercession was his asking the Father for the gift of the Holy Spirit. Peter said it on the day of Pentecost, "Exalted to the right hand of God, he has received from the Father the promised Holy Spirit and has poured out what you now see and hear" (Acts 2:33 NIV). Jesus himself had declared that this would happen as a result of his prayer: "I will ask the Father, and he will give you another Counselor to be with you forever—the Spirit of truth" (Jn 14:16-17 NIV).

Yes, the Holy Spirit had been present in the lives of Old Testament believers. But now he came in a new relationship. "Wait," said Jesus to his disciples. "Wait for what the Father had promised. . . . You shall be baptized with the Holy Spirit not many days from now" (Acts 1:4-5 NASB). These were believers; they certainly had known the Old Testament experience of the Holy Spirit. But now they were standing at a crossroads of history. This relationship to the Holy Spirit would be tied to the exaltation of their Savior; it would be the promise long awaited. It would mean a profound change.

This is the promise spoken of in Hebrews 11:39 that Old Testament believers, though approved for their faith, "did not receive." This is what John the Baptist spoke of in his great summary of what the Messiah would do: "He will baptize you with the Holy Spirit and with fire" (Mt 3:11 NIV).

Do you see how this new presence of the Spirit marked a change of eras? The era was so profoundly new and different that it obliterated tabernacle and temple, Levitical priesthood and sacrifices, ritual feasts and fasts, indeed all the shadows and symbols that pointed toward the reality of the Messiah and his work. Christ's people became the temple of God, because of Christ's powerful and never-ending intercession.

United to Christ

Part of the reality of the new intimacy with the Spirit of God is the new union with the exalted Christ that his presence creates. Jesus said to his disciples, "On that day [that is, the day when the Holy Spirit will come], you will realize that I am in my Father, and you are in me, and I am in you" (Jn 14:20-21 NIV). The Holy Spirit in us is the Spirit of Christ. He creates a living and real bridge between us and the Savior. He seals us in Christ.

We are ready now to understand why all the new concepts under the new covenant come to a focus in the reality of union with Christ. This is the mystery newly revealed. It creates a profound deepening and broadening of the simple death/resurrection/forgiveness gospel of both Old and New Testaments, and strongly calls for a new lifestyle for all Christians of this era.

A key word is *reality*. Because Jesus Christ is alive, gloriously real in his resurrection life and triumph, and because the Holy Spirit of Christ in us is the real bond of union with him, we are actually joined to Jesus Christ. We are joined to all the results of his covenant-keeping and redemptive work: his obedience, his death, his resurrection, his ascension, his glory— all the fruit of his powerful redemption which dwells in his glorified Person. Christ is in us, and we are in Christ. Our entire relationship to the covenants of God is now bound up in our union with the covenant-keeper.

This union is to result in a new lifestyle. Paul describes the change this way, "Now the Lord is the Spirit, and where the Spirit of the Lord is, there is liberty. But we all, with unveiled face beholding as in a mirror the glory of the Lord, are being transformed into the same image from glory to glory, just as from the Lord, the Spirit" (2 Cor 3:17-18 NASB). Actual union with the living Christ has now opened up a new way of operating. This new covenant lifestyle is both mandated and enabled by the union in which we now find ourselves.

United to Each Other

Just as the real presence of the Holy Spirit in Christ's people joins them to him, so the shared presence of the Holy Spirit in all true believers unites us with one another. This union does not depend on performance, exact conformity of doctrine, language or cultural practices. It is not removed by our likes or dislikes of each other, even by our angers or hatreds. It continues through all changes and hassles, even through death itself. We can no more lose it than we can lose our salvation, for it depends on the reality of a new creation in Christ Jesus, a new humanity where there are no divisions, the shared presence of the Holy Spirit in our lives. We now constitute the one body of Christ. Being "under the Law," the condition that divided Jews and Gentiles, is no longer a cause of hostility. We are free and we are one.

In matters of our Christian unity we often live so out of the Spirit who binds us together that it appears as though Christ accomplished nothing. How very important for us to learn to live "by the Holy Spirit"!

All of this is rightly seen in the framework of *covenant,* because it is the high fulfillment of God's design to be with his people. Though it now is a covenant in which we are represented by our Redeemer, it nonetheless involves us because we are in him. It is rightly called a new covenant, not because grace is new to our day, but because the change in our situation is so radical as to create a whole new level of life in God's presence. The substance has replaced the shadows; we are no longer "under the Law" which was a schoolmaster to bring us to Christ; we are in Christ.

Now we must see something of what this opens up to us.

PART II

THE POSSIBILITIES
OF THE NEW

CHAPTER 6

A NEW LEVEL OF PRAYER

I can hear some readers saying, "Prayer! Why prayer first? Here I thought: now, at last, we'll get to some practical application of new covenant teaching! How will all this help me with my work, my family, my schooling? How will it help me heal my hurts, get over my temptations, get along with Dan Brown? Why start with something as insipid as prayer?

To tell the truth, for a long time I didn't have this subject first on my list, either. But it got there eventually when I realized that prayer *comes* first. New covenant living is different precisely because it reflects the exalted, glorified and active Christ, and his heavenly activity started and continues with his intercession. Our entering into his exalted power will start there, too, and will continue there.

Prayer will be primary in our new covenant lifestyle, both private prayer and joint prayer. For most of us this will mean a rather drastic change in our priorities and outlook on prayer. We often look at prayer like the woman who said to me, "Pastor, I've done everything I can think of to do in this situation, and it is absolutely hopeless. I guess all we can do now is pray." In her priorities prayer was the tail end of all effort, what you did only as a final gesture of hopelessness. Under the new covenant prayer is the way of initiating and carrying on all effort.

Joint prayer often has an even lower position in our priorities. I remember sitting in a meeting of church elders discussing whether to start a church prayer meeting. One of the elders, an outspoken man, said with some heat, "I will pray at home, but I see absolutely no point in a public prayer meeting. I will certainly not waste my time coming to one!" Of course, some Christians come to prayer meetings with not much better sense of their importance than this elder had. They perhaps grew up doing it. The church covenant pledged them to attend all the stated meetings of the church. It is part of their loyalty to the church program to be there, and it is quite conceivable that in terms of what happens there it actually *is* a waste of time.

All this changes when we see what Christ has now made possible.

The Prayer Chain
If there is one thing to carry away from the early chapters of this book it is that, as Christians, we have been joined to the living Christ. This is a real, spiritual union. He is there, we are here, but the Holy Spirit joins us to him. This union also means that we are joined to each other in him.

But he is praying; he continuously lives to pray before God's throne. So we are joined spiritually to a praying Christ. Indeed, the staggering thought is that we are joined to his *praying!* The power, accuracy and effectiveness of his praying can begin to permeate ours. The completed work of Jesus has made it possible for us to enter into a simply magnificent chain of intercession.

Think of his end of the chain. There is the exalted Christ himself, our covenant-keeper, presenting the claims of his redemptive work to his Father in our behalf. All that he secured for you and me, for our families, our situations and our churches through his experience at Calvary and through his resurrection, he claims in the presence of the Father. The Father, under the obligations he assumed in covenant relationships, must honor the claims of our Head and Representative. Your forgiveness and acceptance depend on this intercession: he is your Advocate when you sin (1 Jn 2:1-2). Your growth in grace depends on this. The building of the kingdom of Christ, the building of his church depends on this. This is not a one-time-only prayer; it is perpetual. "He always lives to intercede" (Heb 7:25 NIV).

We live our daily lives, go to work, enjoy our homes and families, and have our tragedies, too, but most of the time we are completely oblivious to the fact that every good that we need, every help in trouble, every bit of our security and growth depend on his prayer for us!

The next link in the chain is the Holy Spirit. Jesus and the Father have sent him to us to live and work permanently in us. Since he comes from Jesus and brings things from Jesus to us, it is not really surprising to find that the Holy Spirit in us is the praying Spirit. He "himself intercedes for us with groans that words cannot express. . . . The Spirit intercedes for the saints in accordance with God's will" (Rom 8:26-27 NIV). He does not carry on a separate agenda of prayer in you, that is, separate from Jesus' concerns; his praying is a reflection of Christ's intercession. He brings Jesus' powerful prayers right into your life, as close as your breath.

We are the final link in this prayer chain. So in typical new covenant language, we are exhorted to "pray in the Holy Spirit" (Jude 20 NIV). The presence of the Holy Spirit joins us to the living, interceding Jesus, and our prayers can now begin to reflect his. "He who searches *our* hearts knows the mind of the Spirit, because the Spirit intercedes . . . in accordance with God's will" (Rom 8:27 NIV, italics added). The "mind of the Spirit" here is the believer's mind, under the control and influence of the Holy Spirit. And so the chain is complete.

Perhaps you have heard some say that prayer "in the Spirit" refers entirely to prayer in tongues. Certainly there is such an experience. Paul refers to it in 1 Corinthians 14:14-15, and I will certainly not speak against it. But even in that passage Paul emphasizes prayer that involves the mind. Whatever you think of tongues-praying, remember this principle: the height of Christian experience, indeed of experience with the Holy Spirit, is not the turning off of our personalities, but *fellowship with God.* This is a fellowship of our whole person with God: mind to mind, feelings to feelings, will to will. This is what God desires and what we need. The highest kind of prayer will not be unconscious intercession, but entering into the mind of Christ by the Holy Spirit's help and asking those things that are on his agenda.

This picture of prayer is a new covenant picture. There is nothing like it in the conceptions of the Old Testament. It is part of the unfolded mystery of union with Christ.

Help from the Old Testament

I want to stop here and make sure that we do not underestimate the strong and timeless value of Old Testament teachings about prayer. The Old Testament has some of the finest examples of *worship prayer* to be found anywhere. If you want to grow in this kind of prayer, try studying the magnificent prayer of Hannah after the birth of Samuel (1 Sam 2:1-10), the God-glorifying prayer of David at the gathering of gifts for temple construction (1 Chron 29:10-19), the dedication prayer of Solomon when the temple had been completed (2 Chron 5:12-42). Many psalms are priceless prayers of worship. If you want to learn to express your worship toward God, these and many other portions of the Old Testament will be indispensable.

When you are feeling deep conviction and contrition before the Lord, David's psalm of confession (51) can serve as a heartfelt prayer to him. The Old Testament has some profound *prayers of confession* and repentance like Daniel's prayer of confession on behalf of the entire exiled nation of Israel (Dan 9:4-19), and similar prayers by Ezra and Nehemiah (Ezra 9:5-15; Neh 9:1-37).

The Old Testament also contains some models for *intercession.* Moses' intercession for sinning Israelites at Mount Sinai (Ex 32:31-32) and Abraham's prayer for Sodom and his nephew Lot (Gen 18:22-33) are particularly worth studying. God's calls for intercessors, like those in Isaiah 59:16 and 62:6, will also grip you.

Yet in spite of all these prayer resources, the Old Testament gives no hint of the added marvel of new covenant praying: our union with the great covenant-keeper in his claims before the Father.

The Way Jesus Does His Work Now

I remember a new secretary who came into the office of a Christian organization where I once worked. She came from another state and from a church which really trained its members in putting prayer first. Mind you, we thought we placed a pretty strong emphasis on prayer too. But we would be sitting in conference, smoothly laying out plans for future operations, when we would begin to notice a mildly incredulous look coming over the face of our new secretary. If we asked her why, she would say, "I was just wondering if we shouldn't be covering this with prayer and seeking the Lord's mind on it!" She was uncomfortable whenever the Lord's work was not initiated and carried on in prayer.

If this seems unrealistic, listen to what Jesus has to say: "He who believes in Me, the works that I do shall he do also; and greater works than these shall he do; *because I go to the Father.* And whatever you ask in My name, that will I do, that the Father may be glorified in the Son. If you ask Me anything in My name, I will do it" (Jn 14:12-14 NASB). The experience of prayer that he describes is *enabled* by his "going to the Father," that is, to his exalted state. Christ is promising here that we can be associated with him in his works as glorified Head of the Church. They will be greater works for that very reason, because they are works initiated by Christ, now without the previous limitations of his time here on earth. They will be accompanied by the freedom, glory and power of his present position. We can be associated with him in these greater works by prayer. This is new covenant praying. It is still Jesus Christ doing the works, but he says to you, "You ask, and I'll do it!" Christ's kingdom is built through this kind of prayer.

Stop and think about this a moment. Isn't it amazing that Jesus' program should be described this way—"You ask, and I'll do it"? Here is a crucially important principle for the functioning of our lives, part of the reason why this chapter had to come first in studying the possibilities of new covenant living. Though Jesus Christ has kept the covenant obligation for his people and prays to the Father on our behalf, God desires that these benefits should come into our lives not automatically, but *as we join him in his claiming prayers.*

Even though Jesus did all the work necessary to make us acceptable to God and claimed us from the Father, we did not automatically become converted without an echoing prayer on our part which was enabled by the Holy Spirit.

It is not at all a matter of dreaming up thoughts about what we would like to see God do for us, then asking and receiving what is on our agenda. It is union with Christ in his claims. It is praying "in Jesus' name and for his sake."

The Holy Spirit's Help

This kind of prayer sounds like a great privilege and responsibility, doesn't it? Perhaps your reaction is "That scares me! I don't think I can possibly get into *that* big a scene!" I remember speaking to a prayer meeting on this subject, and when it came time to pray, no one did! I got the distinct impression that everyone felt inadequate for that kind of prayer.

Feeling inadequate for prayer is not all that bad. But if you let it keep you from praying, you have missed some very good news in this picture. The Holy Spirit is here to help us pray! We do not have to plead with him to take an interest in our prayer life! He is the praying Spirit. He is already in motion in that direction and is urging us to put up our sails to catch the wind.

You have thrown a line to a drowning man and are trying to pull him to shore. The current is strong and he is heavy. You realize that you are not strong enough to do it, and the line begins to slip through your hands. Suddenly strong hands are placed over yours and you instantly realize that you are now going to be able to pull him in. "In the same way the Spirit also helps our weakness; for we do not know how to pray as we should" (Rom 8:26 NASB).

Deep, inward fellowship with the Holy Spirit is one of the hallmarks of the new covenant, and nowhere is it stronger than in prayer. *Of course* we can't pray this kind of prayer! That is, we can't on our own. But we can pray in the Spirit. We can call on him for his help and expect it from him. He is not far away; he lives in us! And he lives in us to do this very thing. Believe it! Ask him! Go ahead, *do* it! "Spirit of Jesus, I don't know how to pray; help me know how to think about this situation and what to ask." Then launch out in prayer. You'll soon discover that he is real and so is his help. This is one of the great ways to get to know the Holy Spirit better. There are other things to learn about prayer, but this is one of the basics of new covenant praying.

Praying Together

When we looked at the "mystery of Christ" in Paul's teaching, we saw the importance of the union of believers with each other in Christ. *As Christians we share the presence of the praying Spirit.* By his Spirit we now have the privilege of entering together into Christ's praying. I believe that this kind of joint prayer in the Spirit is one of the most powerful experiences of redemption that we ever have.

Before we look closer at prayer with other Christians, we need to see how our union with other believers enlarges our *private* praying, too. "With all prayer and petition, wrote Paul, "pray at all times in the Spirit, and with this in view, be on the alert with all perseverance and petition for all the saints" (Eph 6:18 NASB). "At all times" does not quite catch the flavor of the Greek word used here for *time*. "At every opportune moment," or "at every strategic juncture" better expresses it. The idea is that there are special moments when prayer is needed by fellow Christians. The next phrase carries this thought further by saying literally: "And for this be watching with all perseverance and petition concerning all the saints." Thus the Holy Spirit alerts to pray for others and calls on us at strategic moments.

This passage does not exhort us to keep mechanically going over a prayer list that contains names of every Christian we know (though prayer lists can be helpful). It teaches rather a Spirit-generated alertness that results in opportune praying. The same Holy Spirit indwells all believers and can easily create this kind of awareness, care and support within the body. This spiritual union with other Christians reaches right into our secret prayer closets and makes powerful prayer support possible.

It is neither necessary nor advisable to think that this sense of need will always come to us by a subjective input of information from the Holy Spirit. More likely it will involve information that has come by ordinary means. The Holy Spirit, however, enables us to evaluate this data in such a way that we sense the need and occasion for prayer. As Christians we should constantly evaluate the data of life with the Holy Spirit's help, so as to be quickly alerted to the need for prayer.

When we actually pray together as Christians, our shared experience of the Holy Spirit, the interceding Spirit, creates a tremendous potential for kingdom action. "Whatever you shall bind on earth," said Jesus, "shall have been bound in heaven; and whatever you loose on earth shall have been loosed in heaven. Again I say to you, that if two of you agree on earth about anything that they may ask, it shall be done for them by My Father who is in heaven. For where two or three have gathered together in My name, there am I in their midst" (Mt 18:18-20 NASB). Christ is with each of us by his Spirit before we come together to pray, but there is a special awareness of him when we are together.

Notice also the strong relationship between heaven and earth. In this kind of prayer a binding and loosing of things on earth can take place which is a reflection of heaven's action. Here is the body of Christ active as agent of the reigning, interceding Christ, bringing into the earthly scene the power of his headship by Spirit-led, joint prayer.

I don't think that we know as much as we need to know about this kind of prayer. The forces of evil seem to be gathering and uniting in a way that challenges us as the people of God more than ever before. We feel powerless to stem the tide or even to protect our children from the molding forces of the world. There is something for us to learn about joint prayer that can bind and loose on earth, and this will perhaps serve to restore our confidence in the reigning power of Jesus Christ. It is exciting to realize that the quorum for this kind of prayer is only *two!*

One summer at a Christian camp, I was in charge of an eight-week collegiate work-study program. One of the applicants we had accepted, a young man with a troubled background, had failed to show up at the beginning, but then came a week late with a Christian girl we knew and loved. She also was going through a rough period of her life. I confronted Joe and said to him, "Take a day to sort out your thoughts and then tell me whether or not you will commit yourself to stay and enter into the program. I want a solid promise from you." After a day he gave me his promise to stay. A day or so later, late in the evening, I heard the report that Joe and his girlfriend were planning to take off the next morning for New Hampshire!

Interestingly enough, that very afternoon I had been discussing the "binding and loosing" passage in Matthew 18 with some friends, and we had been impressed with the need to learn more about this kind of prayer. When I heard about Joe and Martha, I knew immediately that this situation called for something of this kind. I uprooted a couple of junior staff members from their sleep, got them off in a corner of the lounge, and told them what we had to do. They quickly agreed. We called on the Holy Spirit for his help, and the best we knew how we "bound and loosed" for Joe and Martha.

The next morning I passed Joe where he sat on some steps waiting for Martha. I smiled at him and went on about my business. He waited for two or three hours, but Martha never showed up. We found out later that Martha, not one used to sleeping in, had found herself physically unable to get out of bed that morning. In fact, it was after noon before she managed to rise. Both she and Joe stayed the rest of the summer, and each made crucial progress with the Lord. Needless to say I grew in my appreciation of joint prayer.

How can we grow in this? I think for every one person who says, "I have trouble praying by myself" there are ten who say, "I can't pray with others or in public." Even though we have this feeling, the Holy Spirit will help us learn to pray with others. After all, we share the very presence of the interceding Spirit, and it will be important to him to draw us together in prayer. When we step out in faith to do it with his help, not only do we get to know him better, but we will know each other better too.

It is easiest for us to pray with those with whom we have a natural, existing relationship, like our spouses, or other members of a church committee or board, or our children. Finding a prayer-partner to pray with regularly can be a big help. Learn to make joint prayer a part of your fellowship when visiting Christian friends. Usually casual conversation and sharing of news will raise some issues that really need prayer. It ought not to be hard to say, "We talked about so-and-so who is having the problem; let's pray for him before we go." Household prayers, or prayer-partner prayers, can sometimes be profitably organized so that you rotate through various areas of needs: one time on personal futures, another on the church, another on school situations, another time on missions and so on.

Praise

There is extraordinary power in praise, both private and shared with others. Even the Old Testament says that God "inhabits the praises of Israel" (Ps 22:3 KJV). But the new covenant gives us a startling picture of the glorified Jesus. In Hebrews 2:12 these words are put in his mouth: "I will proclaim Thy name to My brethren, in the midst of the congregation I will sing Thy praise" (NASB). Here is Jesus, the Leader of redeemed humanity standing in the midst of his people by his Spirit, instructing them and leading them in their songs of praise! Jesus the songleader! Praise in the Spirit of Christ is unspeakable glory! We must learn to distinguish between so-called praise that is just rah-de-dah noise in which God is not really known, and the kind that makes us aware of the real Lord God. But for all of this, we have a Helper, too.

What we have talked about is just the beginnings of new covenant praying. There is much more to learn about joint prayers of confession, support for evangelism, growth in joint holiness, joint responses to the Word and resistance to the powers of darkness. I do not have the space to enlarge on these here. But I hope that this much you have grasped: Because of your union with Christ, you can enter into his intercession on a high level of power in prayer. The praying Holy Spirit is creating a strong wind of prayer. Put up your sail, and go! And not just alone, but with other Christians! This is the new covenant way of functioning. All else grows out of it.

CHAPTER 7

A NEW LEVEL OF VICTORY

*B*arbara also came to our collegiate program one summer. She looked forward eagerly to the eight-week period but was disappointed when illness forced her to go home after only two weeks. The rest of the summer was filled with illness, aggravated by family conflicts while she recovered. When she went back for her senior year in college, she was still not physically fit and even worse off emotionally. She proceeded to have a rather unhappy time there, too. She found herself irritable over small things, made things rather miserable for her fiance, who attended the same school, and hated herself for the way she was acting.

She was part of a charismatic Christian fellowship group at school and eventually went to the sponsoring minister for counsel. One of his first questions to her, after she had explained her problems, was, "Have you received the baptism in the Spirit?" A slightly impatient look came over her face, and she answered, "Oh, yes. That's not my problem. What I need is some *help!*"

I smiled when I first heard that report, thinking of all the times in counseling sessions when someone had shot down one of my own suggestions. Then I thought more seriously about Barbara's remark. It really doesn't matter that it was in a charismatic setting; the same kind of thing could have happened anywhere. What she was saying was "You can make all the suggestions you want to, but if you don't show me how to handle the evil that is coming out of my own heart, what good is it?" We can tell the sexually tempted man to stay away from pornography, the depressed person to think positively, the overeater to count calories, but if we don't get more basic than that, we will give little help. Even a new experience with the Holy Spirit will not be enough if it does not provide strategic handles for the war against the world, the flesh and the devil.

What we have studied so far about the new covenant now comes to one of its most important tests. Can these understandings actually result in a higher level of victory over evil? I am not going to claim any easy answers in this chapter or a push-button kind of instant power. My own experience tells me that new covenant categories of thought, though clearly present in the New Testament are not familiar patterns of thought, and we prefer what is familiar. To counteract this natural tendency we will need to study what the Scriptures say, pray over them and respond in faith, trusting the Spirit of truth to use the Scriptures to build our understanding. But the fact of the matter is that the new covenant has indeed opened up a higher level of conquest over evil. We must remember, though, that we are not neutral observers on the outside of the problem. We are very much in the middle of it, and we need the Spirit's light and help to understand it.

The Enemies

Scripture clearly teaches that the evil of human sin is rooted in rebellion and independency. Now, don't wince! We are all cut out of this same piece of cloth. Since the Fall the drive for autonomy, that is, the heart-longing to be accountable to no one but ourselves, has been a deep affliction. "Every inclination of his heart is evil from childhood," God said about the human race even after the flood (Gen 8:21 NIV). "They did not listen or pay attention; instead, they followed the stubborn inclinations of their evil hearts" (Jer 7:24 NIV). And God said this about his own people after reminding them of his covenant with them.

Satan is described in the Bible as the archrebel and organizer of rebellion. He is the adversary of God, the god of this world. His world system is a place where love of God and friendship with the world are mutually exclusive (1 Jn 2:15).

God's covenants reflect his desire to be with his people, to have fellowship with them, to have them walking with him. Loving and effective fellowship with God and rebellious independency are at opposite poles. The evils of sin, Satan and this present world have always been the chief obstacles to a covenant fellowship with God. If it is our nature to want to be independent from God, even as Christians, then a covenant of grace, to be effective, must deal with the evils that afflict us. That is just what is implied about the new covenant when Paul says, "Live by the Spirit, and you will not gratify the desires of the sinful nature" (Gal 5:16 NIV).

The Old Testament View

How did Old Testament believers understand the struggle with sin and evil? Let's give them as much credit as we can, and yet ask ourselves, "Do we know anything more than they did?"

The Old Testament believer certainly understood something of the role of repentance, confession and forgiveness: "Then I acknowledged my sin to you and did not cover up my iniquity. I said, 'I will confess my trangressions to the LORD'—and you forgave the guilt of my sin" (Ps 32:5 NIV). They were constantly reminded, too, that forgiveness was dependent on atonement, even though it was a preliminary picture that was before them in the animal sacrifices and the priesthood. They also understood that Scripture had a role in keeping sin under control, "I have hidden your word in my heart that I might not sin against you" (Ps 119:11 NIV). That these statements are in the form of prayers shows us that Old Testament believers knew something of the need for prayer in contending with evil. Most prayers in this department seem to center on the need for forgiveness, deliverance from trouble or the continued favor of

God, but occasionally they pleaded for help to overcome their sinfulness: "Direct my footsteps according to your word; let no sin rule over me" (Ps 119:133 NIV).

We get the impression that victory over sin for Old Testament believers involved staying close to God through his Word and prayer, engaging faithfully in the Levitical system of atonement, obtaining forgiveness promptly, asking for circumstances which would be favorable for a walk with God, and above all, from Moses' time on, seeking to cope strongly with the Law. In their fellowship with God, and especially in their participation in praise and worship, they sometimes shone brightly. There is much true righteousness and holiness in the best of old covenant experience, much that challenges our present faith.

Well, how do we stack up against that? Do we know something significantly more than that in our personal fight against sin? If we do, it is because of new covenant understandings.

The New Covenant Way

Under the new covenant we find a new intimacy with the Holy Spirit which says that help is closer at hand than before. There are startling new insights into the accomplishments of Jesus in conquering sin, Satan and the world. Above all, there is the new reality of union with Christ which the New Testament Scriptures apply directly to the problem of overcoming evil. These are new focuses for our faith and action in this war.

Let us look at a most unusual passage of Scripture, Romans 7:1-6. It gets to the heart of the matter beautifully. This is the place where Paul uses the analogy of two marriages to describe what Christ did for us and the significance of our union with him. Briefly the teaching is this: a woman is bound by law to her husband as long as he lives. His death, however, frees her from that bond and enables her to enter into a second marriage. The two marriages are used to represent two large spheres of reality in our union with Christ.

Consider the two areas being described. The first one, represented by the first marriage, is an area in which Law held sway (Rom

7:4). It is a sphere in which "we were in the flesh," and "the sinful passions, which were aroused by the Law, were at work in the members of our body" (Rom 7:5). The outcome of this operation of sin was "to bear fruit for death" (Rom 7:5). This area is described as the "oldness of the letter," or as the NIV has it, "the old way of the written code" (Rom 7:6).

The second area describes us as being joined "to Him who was raised from the dead" (Rom 7:4). The result of this: "that we might bear fruit for God" (Rom 7:4). In this sphere we are "released from the Law" and we "serve in newness of the Spirit" (Rom 7:6, all NASB). The first area is one in which evil, law and death operate; the second is one in which release, new life, freedom and newness of the Spirit are to be found.

"You also were made to die to the Law *through the body of Christ*," Paul says, "that you might be joined to another, to Him who was raised from the dead" (Rom 7:4, italics added). The expression "through the body of Christ" is especially important. Since it is contrasted with "Him who was raised from the dead" in this verse, it must refer to the *dead Christ*. Plainly implied is that the whole sphere of evil to which we are naturally bound—our first marriage in the analogy—was somehow completely taken over by Jesus. He *became* the first husband and died to break that union.

Just think what this *means!* How completely Jesus embraced the whole sphere of evil is stated positively in other Scriptures: "God made him who had no sin *to be sin* for us" (2 Cor 5:21 NIV, italics added); "that by the grace of God he might taste death for everyone" (Heb 2:9 NIV). He was permitted to experience the full weight of Satanic oppression (see Lk 22:53); when he died even the world was crucified (Gal 6:14). Under the full rigor of the Law he went down into death, taking into the grave with him the whole first creation, marred and bound by evil. The results are total. As far as his person is concerned, he put away sin by the sacrifice of himself (Heb 10:26). He abolished death (2 Tim 1:10). He destroyed Satan (Heb 2:14). He overcame the world (Jn 16:33). The scope of these statements is so large we are compelled to realize that the whole realm of evil was embraced and overcome by Jesus' death.

But Paul is saying even more in Romans 7:4. He is saying that "You, my brethren, also were made to die to the Law through the body of Christ." His embracing of the sphere of evil involved his embracing of us. The union is as close as a marriage, and his death is our release. We are freed to enter into a second marriage: our partner, the risen Christ. All that we long for and need is gloriously present in the living Jesus.

This Romans 7 passage is surely one of the basic statements of union with Christ in the New Testament. It is truly magnificent in its breadth and implications. It is at the heart of the mystery which had not been revealed in Old Testament times.

Just as the gospel has the dual centers of Christ's death and his resurrection, so union with Christ centers there too. The power of both the death and resurrection reside in the victorious Christ now, and by his Spirit we are joined to him. This paves the way for a new and powerful coping with evil in our lives and situations.

Mental Hocus Pocus?

Perhaps this kind of talk seems very grand and unreal to you. After all, as a Christian you are distressingly aware that evil still operates in your human nature. You know that you are still a target for the attacks of a real and powerful devil. You know that eventually you face death, and even now often have times of spiritual deadness. You are surrounded by an evil world, and its allurements and traps are very real. Am I trying to tell you that somehow by thinking this way about Christ, you can pretend that the real evil around you isn't there? Psychological self-hypnosis doesn't sound like real help, even when it is dressed up in doctrinal clothing!

But wait! There is a large difference between faith and mental self-deception. The eye of faith, instructed by the Word, sees Jesus as living and real, victorious in just the ways the Bible says he is. It sees the indwelling Holy Spirit as real, the actual presence of the living God with us. The eye of faith sees union with Christ, not merely as an ideal, or an idea, or an exercise in pretense; it sees the bridge of union as every bit as real as any of the evil that's on the other side in this war. The *fact* that the almighty Spirit of God, since the completion of Jesus' redemptive work, now abides with us in a deeply inward way to administer the triumph of Christ should fill us with new hope, no matter how realistically we are aware of the curse of evil.

Holy Spirit Demonstrations

Jesus gave a decided new covenant setting to a remarkable teaching recorded in John 16: "But I tell you the truth, it is to your advantage that I go away; for if I do not go away, the Helper will not come to you; but if I go, I will send Him to you. And He, when He comes, will convict the world concerning sin, and righteousness, and judgment; concerning sin, because they do not believe in Me; and concerning righteousness, because I go to the Father, and you no longer behold Me; and concerning judgment, because the ruler of this world has been judged" (Jn 16:7-11 NASB).

Notice the direct connection between Jesus' return to the Father and the coming of the "Helper." This echoes an earlier statement in John: "the Spirit was not yet given, because Jesus was not yet glorified" (7:39 NASB). This is talking about the new relationship to the Holy Spirit which will reflect Jesus' exaltation.

But what has the Holy Spirit come to do, and where does he do it? The activity of the Holy Spirit described here has a very particular location—us! "I will send Him to *you*," Jesus said. When he has come to us, he will do all these things. We are the operating center for this work of the Holy Spirit in convicting the world. He intends to do this work by setting up effective and convincing demonstrations in our lives that will then influence the world around us.

There is to be a demonstration in us regarding *sin*. Jesus' explanation: "concerning sin because they do not believe in me." Jesus has sent the Holy Spirit to us to set up a convincing demonstration of true faith in Christ. It is to be so convincing that the person in the world in whom the Holy Spirit is working will become aware of the truly fatal sin of not believing in Christ, because of the impact of our faith!

The Holy Spirit has also come to us to set up a demonstration of righteousness. Jesus' explanation: "because I go to the Father, and you no longer behold Me." While Jesus lived here, he visibly showed what righteousness is. Now he would no longer be visible to the world. He will be showing his righteousness through us. We are now to be that convincing demonstration of righteousness to the world!

The third demonstration is about judgment. The Holy Spirit has come to us from Jesus to convince the world of judgment. What judgment? Jesus explanation: "because the ruler of this world has been judged." By the Holy Spirit's work the mighty victory that Jesus achieved over Satan and evil is to be demonstrated convincingly in *us*—right before the eyes of an evil, Satan-dominated world!

As we have said, these victories over evil have already been secured in the person of Christ. Sin, death and Satan have no more access to him at all, and he has left this world. But we still live in the realm where evil operates. The Holy Spirit is not only our connection with Jesus, like a lifeline that will eventually pull us out of the sinkhole, but he intends to show the world what has been done by Jesus by demonstrating it in us right here. What a marvel! Here we are still sinners by nature, still attacked and easily vulnerable to the enemy, still living in a dangerously attractive world where concentrated patterns and coalitions of evil operate and try to swallow us up, but we are to be oases of light in a dark world. We are deeply indwelt by the sovereign God, the Holy Spirit, who joins us to the triumphant Christ.

How to Get This to Work

So here we are, with a natural tie to the sphere of evil and a spiritual tie (just as real) to the new creation in Christ. We obviously need a strong and continuous work of grace that will increasingly weaken the hold of the old and overcome its dark ways and will establish more and more the ways of Christ in our experience. The good news is that our union with Jesus and the inward activity of the Holy Spirit provide the way for this to happen. John 16 has to mean that. If the Holy Spirit has come to set up such demonstrations, he is able to do it.

Keep in mind the *order* of the two "marriages" of Romans 7. You are joined first to the dead body of Christ, the dead husband, then to the risen Christ, the second husband. You are in touch with all the power and effectiveness of Christ in both areas: first with the power of his death and the release that this brings, then with his new life. The Holy Spirit intends to conform you to Christ's dying in order to conform you to his resurrection life. In fact, this is almost exactly what Paul wrote to the Philippians: "I want to know Christ and the power of his resurrection and the fellowship of sharing in his sufferings, becoming like him in his death, and so, somehow, to attain to the resurrection from the dead" (3:10-11 NIV). Notice again the cause-and-effect impact of the order: being conformed to his death opens up the experience of his resurrection.

I remember well the moment the significance of this order in Philippians 3:11 dawned on me. The Holy Spirit wanted me to die with Christ in order to open up his life to me. I must join him in death in order to join him in life. Or to put it another way: the Holy Spirit must clear away the junk of my rebellion so that he may reign with Christ's power in my life. My part is to respond in faith and agree actively to this procedure.

Listen to how Paul puts this in Romans: "Don't you know that all of us who were baptized into Christ Jesus were baptized into his death? We were therefore buried with him through baptism into death in order that, just as Christ was raised from the dead through the glory of the Father, we too may live a new life" (6:3-4 NIV).

A process is to take place in our lives which involves a powerful infusion of both death and life from Christ. When the Holy Spirit came to dwell in us, he encountered at the core of our being our rebel tendencies, our desire to be independent. This created a sharp conflict deep within us—the living God resisted by, and resisting, our god-complex. "The sinful nature desires what is contrary to the Spirit, and the Spirit what is contrary to the sinful nature. They are in conflict with each other" (Gal 5:17 NIV). This conflict is still going on. In order to clear the way for his own desires to prevail in our experience, he must first apply death to our independency. He brings this to us straight from the inexhaustible storehouse of Christ's death, to which he has joined us.

Our Part

There was a strategic lesson in the preceding chapter of this book which now becomes vital to understanding our part in this process. The lesson was that though Christ has accomplished all these things for us, and though he lays claim to them in his heavenly intercession, they do not grow in our experience automatically. We must join our prayer to his, responding in faith and prayer. His prayer must find an echo in our claim, before our experience will begin to reflect his victory.

For us to experience Christ's victory over sin, we must make our claim of death to sin by the enabling of the Holy Spirit. Romans 6:11 and 8:13 go together to show clearly the faith/prayer response we must make: "Count yourselves dead to sin but alive to God in Christ Jesus. . . . If by the Spirit you put to death the misdeeds of the body, you will live" (NIV).

Think back a moment to Ken and Shelley. One of the things Ken said to me in that first conversation was, "I think I will die if I cannot have her." He was closer to the truth than he realized, except that he had the order wrong. He needed to die *so that* he would not need to have her. What he later realized was that Christ had already encountered and conquered his problem and provided the death for him to die. The Holy Spirit's presence joined him to that provision of death along with the power to make it real. Ken's personal need for Shelley was immensely strong. He could see no possible way out of his bind. When he saw that his union with Jesus brought him directly in touch with the virtue and power of death to his own independent way, when he saw that the Holy Spirit could strengthen his will to choose that, he saw hope for the first time. He responded in prayer along those lines and found that power real. He experienced death and then resurrection. Our faith often needs some new covenant instruction, before we can respond knowledgeably to Christ and find the experience of victory.

But we must remember that this conformation to Jesus' death is only a means to an end. We do not dwell on the death side of things. As the power of our independency is broken we are free to experience fellowship with the living Christ, a marvelously lively and joyous reality, and this is what really characterizes our life, rather than an unhealthy morbidity.

This is not wishful praying! We are not praying, "Lord, I wish you would please help me in my fight against evil." Rather, on the ground of Christ's victory over the very evil we face, on the ground of our union with him in his death and resurrection, on the ground of his effective intercession for us, and with the sure knowledge that the Holy Spirit has come to bring Christ's power into our lives, we lay claim to it by faith. We choose decisively our place with Jesus in death to all our independency, our right to go our own way. We ask the Holy Spirit to make it effective and count on him to do it. Because of our place in our covenant-keeper, we have a *right* to expect results. He has all the death and all the life we need to be able to walk with God. Dying opens the door to living.

Precisely the same potential is opened up for us in facing all kinds of evil. Christ has conquered *Satan*. He claims for us the fruit of his triumph. By the Holy Spirit's help, making sure first that we are ourselves submitted to God, we resist the devil in the authority of Jesus Christ and see him flee (Jas 4:7). "The God of peace will soon crush Satan *under your feet*" (Rom 16:20 NIV). Is this some new triumph? No, it is simply the application of Christ's victory through us by the power of his Spirit.

The New Testament has much to say about us and the world. But our victory over the world is based on the same new covenant principles. As Jesus approached the cross, he said, "Now is the time for judgment on this world; now the prince of this world will be driven out" (Jn 12:31 NIV); and again, "In this world you will have trouble. But take heart! I have overcome the world" (Jn 16:33 NIV). Paul makes clear that by our participation in Calvary's triumph we overcome the world: "May I never boast except in the cross of our Lord Jesus Christ, through which the world has been crucified to me, and I to the world" (Gal 6:14 NIV).

The victory we achieve over this world's evils will be extended by exactly the same new covenant dynamics that we have been talking about. We must use the weapon of the cross against those elements of our own nature that respond to the world's temptations. We may often have to resist the prince of this world when we sense that he is trying to mount an attack on us from the world. But we do it in union with Christ by the power of the Holy Spirit, and with much prayer.

As we have noted before, the mystery of union with Christ is not just an individual matter. A strong, almost prevailing dimension of it is the union of all true believers in Christ. Victory over sin, Satan and the world can therefore include a corporate reality.

In the Holy Spirit's unity we can find great help from our brothers and sisters in the fight against our old nature. United resistance to the devil is much stronger. We lose some of our hold on victory when we fail to realize the potential help that can come from Christ's body. It is actually one of the ways he approaches us. It is also true that corporate sins afflict Christians, as well as corporate struggles with the Satanic kingdom and with the world. These require knowledge of how to function together in the shared presence of the Holy Spirit.

Strong Hope

Maybe you have been knocked around a bit in your Christian life. I trust that what we have been talking about has brought you new hope. These concepts are really filled with hope, because they are based on realities of the greatest significance. Jesus Christ really has embraced the whole extent of your problem with evil. He really has conquered all that is against you, and today he stands alive and free in great glory. By the indwelling presence of the Holy Spirit you have a real union with Jesus. Although his presence in you indeed results in a sharp contest between him and your sin-nature, his presence brings real power to bear on your need. It should be comforting to realize that he is in conflict with your sinfulness. You don't have to twist his arm to get him to take interest in your fight with sin. He already has a gale blowing against it. Put up your sail and get moving.

Here is a call to a transformed life. Here is glorious power which makes being "under the Law" no longer necessary. As you make the faith-responses Scripture calls for, you are among those who "are being transformed into his likeness with ever-increasing glory, which comes from the Lord, who is the Spirit" (2 Cor 3:18 NIV).

A caution here. Let us not misunderstand this matter of the Law. The standards of righteousness set by God are not discarded under the new arrangement. What God expects is still of great importance to you. The new covenant realities exist "in order that the righteous requirements of the law might be fully met in us, who do not live according to the sinful nature but according to the Spirit" (Rom 8:4 NIV). Christ's complete obedience to his Father now is brought to your life by the Holy Spirit. But now you live in the substance of his accomplishment, not in the shadows that pointed ahead to it. Now unlimited power touches your weakness. New covenant Scriptures not only reveal this, but show you how to take hold of these things by faith.

The study of new covenant doctrines could sound awfully heavy and full of systems and structures. Your Christian life might loom as a terribly complicated thing. But don't forget that we are talking about a covenant, and the goal of covenants is fellowship with God. The new covenant means a closer fellowship with God than was possible before. Walking in the new covenant is really a matter of responding personally to God who indwells us, of knowing Jesus better, of operating in the simplicity of unhindered love. The maintenance of this relationship with sensitivity calls for instructed responses. But they are personal responses to a Lord who wants to be known—simple and not complex. May it be so for you.

CHAPTER 8

—

A NEW LEVEL
OF GUIDANCE

—

Charlie got off the bus drunk and smoking like a furnace. I suppose some would say that he was exhibiting the unconquerable human spirit, but his appearance was disappointing to me, his pastor. Charlie was in his late sixties and had been an alcoholic all his adult life. In fact, when he was ten years old, he had gotten into the family wine barrel before school and was sent home drunk.

I had invested a lot in Charlie. One year I went to his house at 6:45 every morning from Easter until Christmas to try to get him off to work sober and in touch with the Lord. I'd had lots of opportunity to study Charlie and his ways of thinking. One theory that I had gradually developed was that there was some kind of connection between his addiction to tobacco and his alcoholism.

One reason I was particularly discouraged when Charlie got off the bus that day was that he was arriving home from a three-month stay in a colony for rehabilitating alcoholics. He had been required to commit himself for a minimum of three months, and he stayed not one day over the minimum. The reason: they wouldn't let him smoke cigarettes while he was there and he was dying for a smoke. He hated his alcoholism, but he loved his smoking.

That night, when he had sobered up a little, I talked with Charlie. He was a professing Christian, indeed could tell you a delightful story of how he had accepted Christ as a boy. As we talked, I said to him, "Charlie, I am not going to tell you what you ought to do. But suppose for a moment that the Lord himself told you to stop smoking. Would you do it?" Charlie's answer was immediate: "I won't even ask him," he said, "because I don't intend to stop." Chalk one up for Charlie's honesty.

But his answer shook me to my shoes. Immediately to my mind came Christ's words: "Not every one that saith unto me, Lord, Lord, shall enter into the kingdom of heaven; but he that doeth the will of my Father which is in heaven" (Mt 7:21 KJV). I am convinced that in the depths of every true Christian's heart the Spirit of God has planted a desire for God's will that usually keeps him from speaking out as boldly as Charlie had. I cannot judge Charlie's eternal destiny. What a person says under circumstances like his is happily not always the bottom line of his heart.

Nevertheless, the issues of a divine purpose for our lives and how we are to achieve it are large issues. If we are sensitive and committed Christians, we long to live purposefully to the glory of God.

Sometimes a person may have a concept of God's sovereignty that greatly reduces his sense of accountability for his actions and choices. If everything is foreordained, and all our actions are governed by the will of God, why should we need to seek his will at all? Why read the Bible? Why pray? Why trouble our minds over the evil we do? It will all conform to his purpose, won't it? This may sound logical, but it certainly doesn't sound biblical. A great many Scriptures make it plain that God deals with us genuinely within our time-frame and circumstances and calls on us to live responsibly according to what pleases him.

He does not sit over us and say, "It is a matter of indifference to me whether you do this or that; in either case my will will prevail and I will be glorified." Rather we hear him saying, "All day long I have held out my hands to an obstinate people. . . . I take no pleasure in the death of the wicked, but rather that they turn from their ways and live. Turn! Turn from your evil ways! Why will you die, O house of Israel?" (Is 65:2; Ezek 33:11 NIV).

If the redemptive path that God holds before his people means that much to him, it surely should mean a great deal to us. Along this path we need his leading and teaching. We do not walk on it automatically. Only in fellowship with him do we find it. Both Testaments are full of this idea: "I will instruct you and teach you in the way you should go; I will counsel you and watch over you. Do not be like the horse or the mule, which have no understanding" (Ps 32:8-9 NIV). "Trust in the LORD with all your heart and lean not on your own understanding; in all your ways acknowledge him [Hebrew: 'know him'], and he will make your paths straight" (Prov 3:5-6 NIV). "Since the day we heard about you, we have not stopped praying for you and asking God to fill you with the knowledge of his will through all spiritual wisdom and understanding" (Col 1:9 NIV).

Old Covenant Guidance

How did Old Testament believers find God's will? As we try to answer this question, we must remember that in that era, as in any era, God's ability to give guidance is far more important than his people's ability to get it. Since he truly is a God who desires to be known, loved and followed, he takes the initiative in making his will known. We are not eager followers trying to get him to pay attention to us, trying to make him willing to unfold his mind to us, but he is an all-wise Father who is sovereignly capable of breaking through to the consciousness of his children and who wants to. This is a comforting thought in any age.

He used many ways in Old Testament times to direct his people. At first, there was no written revelation of God at all. Only gradually did the Bible become a factor in guidance. Nevertheless, God spoke to his people through all ages. He spoke with Adam, with Noah, with Abraham and his descendants. He used dreams with Joseph, angels with Jacob, a mistreated ass with Balaam. Priests used the Urim and Thummim (apparently some part of the priestly vestments) to find God's will. God led his people through the wilderness by a cloud and fiery pillar. Lots were cast, as when the Promised Land was divided among the twelve tribes. Often God spoke directly, as he did to the child Samuel in the night. At other times he spoke through the prophets in such a unique way that it resulted in the formation of Scripture. Then there was Gideon and his fleeces, too. Without parallel was the revelation written in stone on Mount Sinai.

As the written Word enlarged from Moses' time onward, it became more of a factor in guidance. It was especially needed as a reminder of the laws and statutes under which all old covenant believers were bound: "Do not let this Book of the Law depart from your mouth; meditate on it day and night, so that you may be careful to do everything written in it" (Josh 1:7-8 NIV). This sometimes became a deep inward experience for the committed believers who hid it in their hearts: "Your word is a lamp to my feet and a light for my path" (Ps 119:105 NIV).

What becomes clear about Old Testament times is that God expected obedience to his will, took many steps and used many means to show a path to his people. And after Sinai they were clearly under the Law. How then is our experience of God's guidance different from that of Old Testament saints?

New Covenant Guidance

Ephesians is a mature expression of new covenant truth, unfolding the previously hidden mystery. There you hear Paul describing the kind of new covenant life now open to believers. Listen: "You were once darkness, but now you are light in the Lord. Live as children of light (for the fruit of the light consists in all goodness, righteousness and truth) and *find out what pleases the Lord.* Have nothing to do with the fruitless deeds of darkness, but rather expose them. . . . 'Wake up, O sleeper, rise from the dead, and Christ will shine on you.' Be very careful, then, how you live—not as unwise but as wise, making the most of every opportunity, because the days are evil. Therefore, do not be foolish, *but understand what the Lord's will is.* . . . Be filled with the Spirit" (Eph 5:8-18 NIV, italics added).

Notice that the Word here commands us to understand God's will and places responsibility on us to wake up to it. What really sets this passage into the new covenant level are the references to Christ and to the Holy Spirit: "Christ will shine on you. . . . Be filled with the Holy Spirit." This is not just a fanciful way of talking about Jesus. Christ was far too real to the apostle Paul for him to do that. Light on the will of God streams to us from the living exalted Lord, if we are spiritually awake enough to receive it. The Holy Spirit guides us into it, if we are sufficiently filled with him. You may be certain of this: there is indeed a new covenant level of guidance into the will of God for your life.

Jesus' Fulfillment of God's Will

As the second and last Adam, Jesus stood as representative for the human race just as Adam had before him. Adam failed to obey; Christ did not. Jesus spoke often of the fact that he *always* did the will of his Father. His entire earthly life was lived in perfect obedience, even though that path led him to a cross. Obedience to the Father's will is central to his function as our covenant-keeper.

Then in his death Jesus grappled with all the sinful rebellion of the human race, yours and mine. This included all the deadly separation from the life of God that characterizes us, all the Satanic tyrannies and deceptions that trap us in a path contrary to the Father's will. He conquered them by his death and came out of the grave free from them. He had no need to do these things for himself; he did them for us.

Jesus so identified himself with those for whom he died that you can almost say that he not only died *for* us, but *as* us. We may rightly think of the things that happened to him as having happened to us. Most important, Jesus secured a total victory over all the enemies that rob *us* of a walk in the will of God. In his resurrection newness he has secured the total plan for our lives. In him, it is perfectly created and worked out.

In his present intercession before the heavenly tabernacle the Lord presents his sacrifice and intercedes for us that we might enter into the full effect of what he has done—of what happened to us in him. He has sent the Holy Spirit to us to seal us in a real union with himself. We are also, then, sealed in a union with the plan of God for our lives. The Holy Spirit is with us also to be the administrator of Christ's triumph in the here and now of our daily life. So we, through the Holy Spirit, are in touch with the plan that Christ has secured for our lives.

Is it any wonder that Paul said the Holy Spirit would lead the children of God? He is not an independent guide, activating some plan for us that is his own initiating. He is operating in the new covenant union as the agent of Christ's redemption, unfolding to us what Christ has secured for us. He brings to our heart the very attitude of obedience that characterized our covenant-keeper. Do you have trouble saying, "Not my will but thine be done?" Well, take courage! Jesus has said it already for you and therefore the Holy Spirit can help you echo his mind.

Paul knew that his life plan came to him from Jesus. He said to the Ephesian elders, "I do not consider my life of any account as dear to myself, in order that I may finish my course, and the ministry *which I received from the Lord Jesus*" (Acts 20:24 NASB, italics added). We saw before how Paul had some unique dealings with the Lord Jesus, and we might be tempted to think that only a few special leaders of the church receive this kind of awareness of a plan for their lives from him. But what Jesus has secured for us by his redemption is every bit as complete as for Paul. The mode of communication may vary in some details, but the essential truth remains. This is new covenant privilege, and it is ours as well as his. In the famous passage of Ephesians 4, where Paul describes the exalted Christ giving gifts to the church in the form of people with unique ministries, he ends up by having every part of the body contributing ministry to the whole—and that includes you and me.

Paul wrote this instruction to Timothy: "Guard the good deposit that was entrusted to you—guard it with the help of the Holy Spirit who lives in us" (2 Tim 1:14 NIV). The Greek word translated "deposit" means a trust, here something entrusted to Timothy. Literally the verse reads, "Guard the beautiful trust through the Holy Spirit who lives in us." The deposit is not the Holy Spirit himself, for it is by the Holy Spirit that he is admonished to guard it. Nor is it simply the factual gospel for Timothy to keep intact. Rather it is the commission given to Timothy by Christ to complete—the beautiful intention of the Lord to make special use of Timothy's life—the plan given him in trust. Throughout the letters to Timothy, Paul seems concerned to help the young man overcome his fears and fulfill this divinely ordained role. The Holy Spirit is present to enable this, but Timothy has responsibility too.

Our Responsibility

We indeed have a course to follow, and Christ's Spirit is with us to unfold it and enable us to walk in it. Several factors will need to be clear in our minds when we consider just how God's plan is to be carried out in our lives. Overall our major responsibility is to maintain a fellowship with the Holy Spirit that will result in "guarding our trust." As we have said several times now, the things that Jesus claims for us before the Father do not automatically become part of our experience. We must respond in faith, prayer and action, as assisted by the Holy Spirit.

We need to have a careful understanding of the role of Scripture in guidance. Even in Old Testament times, Scripture was never simply a *rulebook* for guidance. It has always been the revelation of the living God and a means to bring people to himself. To say that Scripture is *covenant* is to say precisely this. But the impact of Law during the Mosaic covenant time was so heavy that there must have been great pressure to see the Bible only as a compendium of rules for life situations.

Many still make that mistake today. They feel that the whole process of finding God's will is simply to find Scriptures that tell us what to do in given situations. Of course the Bible is not going to tell you whether you ought to marry Mary Jane, or whether you should go to State U., or whether you should accept the nomination for treasurer of First Baptist Church, or play football your first year in college, or change jobs, or buy the kids new shoes. Still some people feel uneasy about going beyond the letter of the Bible for guidance. Too dangerous, they say. And besides it would somehow be treating the Bible as though it was not sufficient for us.

Actually the sufficiency of the Bible doesn't lie in that direction, as though God revealed there every bit of guidance that he wants us to have. If that were true, it would mean that he didn't care whether you married Mary Jane or which way you went in most of life's decisions. Actually the sufficiency of the Bible lies in its completeness as the revelation of the way to him. It must always be present in your life to build, test, guard and maintain your fellowship with God. Of course God wants you to know whether or not you should decide to go into the pastorate. Yet the Bible alone is not going to reveal a yes for you and a no for someone else by its teachings, except perhaps in broad categories. What he wants instead is that by means of the Word and prayer and daily growth in fellowship with him you would come to the place where he can call you to the pastorate or not, with a reasonable degree of assurance on your part.

We must indeed be careful not to be oversubjective in our fellowship with God, but the Bible should help us grow in real wisdom and the ability to sort out the factors of a decision, without being unstable or whimsical. If you are one of those people who love C. S. Lewis's Narnia Tales, you will remember in *The Voyage of the Dawn Treader* how the travelers who were approaching Aslan's country by sea found that the water in the ocean was fresh and sweet, and as they drank it they were more and more able to endure the increasing brilliance of that land. So the steady use of Scripture will enable you to walk in Christ's light.

Our enjoyment of new covenant guidance will rest in the nature of fellowship with God. God's desire to be known, understood and loved implies full function of *our beings* as well as his. He does not desire puppets; he desires persons with whom he can interact— mind to mind, feelings to feelings, will to will. It is not a fellowship of equals, but it is a fellowship of whole persons.

In Romans 8:16 Paul says, "The Spirit Himself bears witness with our spirit that we are children of God" (NASB). The English word "with" is rather uncertain. Does it mean that the Holy Spirit bears witness "to" our spirit, or does it mean that he bears witness "along with" our spirit? The difference could be quite significant. In the first case it might imply that the witness of the Spirit ordinarily comes to us as direct interventions into our minds, while we remain passively receptive. The second case suggests a more active involvement of our minds, an occupation with the data of a situation and a fellowship with the Holy Spirit in that process. The Greek original definitely favors the second idea, a mutual looking at the situation. The Holy Spirit is able to associate his assurance with our evaluative process, and a solid, workable conviction is born.

I believe that this is the normal manner of guidance for us as Christians. While it would not be right for us to say that God never could or would place a leading in our minds without our conscious involvement in the process (after all, who are we to tell God what he can and cannot do?), yet the norm is fellowship with the Holy Spirit in these considerations. The height of redemptive experience is not the turning off of our personalities and the turning on of the Holy Spirit. The height of Christian experience is walking with God.

The Role of Other Christians

Once more, the fact that union with Christ is not simply an individual experience, but a group-sharing of the Holy Spirit's presence, says something to us about following God's will. The body of Christ can and should experience corporate guidance. Together groups of Christians should be able to consider the factors in joint decisions and know the fellowship of the Holy Spirit in finding the plan of Christ. This is not the same as democracy, since majorities can be out of touch with the Spirit of God. They should listen prayerfully to minorities! Also other Christians can help us check out the choices we make as individuals, when we need additional assurance. Just be careful not to depend on other Christians to find God's will for you!

I shall always be deeply grateful to God that when Joyce and I were married in 1946, we already had the solid conviction that we could get down together before God and discover his plan for our family life. It has never been necessary to "pull rank" on each other or to make decisions in which we did not agree. We have not, of course, been infallible in discerning God's will, but we have lived with reasonable assurance that we were following the overall plan of God, and we have lived at peace. We have shared the same Holy Spirit and his leading.

Practical Suggestions on Guidance

In day-to-day decision-making, here are some factors to keep in mind.

Believe on the basis of God's Word that the finished work of Christ does contain the plan for your life, and for your life with other Christians. Believe that the covenant Head is interceding right now with the Father to secure light on your path according to his will. Believe that the Holy Spirit is here to implement that very plan and is well able to do it. Believe that your union with Christ has put you in touch with the mind of Christ. And what if you have trouble believing these things? Then take the Scriptures that tell you these truths and ask the Holy Spirit to make them real to your faith. With his presence in you— with the kind of winds that come from him—you do not need to stay becalmed. You never start from scratch. The triune God is for you.

Maintain fellowship with God. Far more important than techniques of guidance is your close fellowship with Christ and his Spirit. Here persistent use of Scripture is vitally important, as well as prayer, praise, fellowship with other Christians and exercising your gifts in ministry.

Deal with obstacles to guidance. Fellowship with God must involve submission and commitment. On many occasions you will need to wield the weapon of Christ's death against those biases and desires which can lead you astray. Satan is a clever deceiver and sometimes must be resisted as we make a decision. Your union with Christ provides you with authority to do this.

In prayer examine and evaluate the facts of a decision. While you may remain open for supernormal ways the Lord may approach you, do not neglect the responsible use of your mind and the prayerful work of evaluation which is done in true fellowship with God.

Both as a safeguard for personal decisions and as the right way to conduct kingdom business, *learn to function under the Holy Spirit's direction with fellow believers.* If your spouse is a Christian, by all means start there and discover together the Lord's will for your family. If you face a difficult decision, ask other Christians to pray with you about it. They don't have to tell you what the answer is, but great strength and wisdom often grows just from the process of being united by the Holy Spirit in prayer.

I love the New English Bible translation of Ephesians 5:8. We quoted the NIV earlier in this chapter, "Live as children of light." The NEB says that as Christians we ought to be those who are *"at home in daylight."* This is your privilege in union with Jesus. Go for it!

CHAPTER 9

A NEW LEVEL OF UNITY

I *think it was Richard Lovelace whom I first heard describe the way we often* sit in church. I thought it was terribly funny until I thought about it more. He said that we often sit in church as though we each were inside the bottom of a cylinder, just our size, that reached from our seat right up to God. Economic necessity, perhaps, forces us to share the same auditorium, but our individual cylinders allow us to concentrate on God without being bothered by other Christians.

Being a proper Bostonian by background, I have done a great deal of cylinder-sitting in my time. It still comes quite natural to me. Well, yes, I realize the Bible calls that person next to me my brother, but I really don't know much about him—that is, nothing *personal.* To be honest with you, I really don't *want* to! It hardly seems right to be prying into his affairs. Of course I hope he's doing all right, but that's really between him and God. I came here to worship, not to think about him.

This is hardly a new covenant attitude. When Paul discussed the revelation of the mystery hidden from previous ages, he empha- •

sized our corporate union with Christ even more than our individual union. Perhaps this was because of his concern about relationships between Jews and Gentiles and the serious crisis this issue brought upon the church of his day. In any case, he made strong statements about the union which now exists among believers because of the shared presence of the Holy Spirit.

In any study of the new covenant we cannot overlook the New Testament emphasis on the relationships and interactions of believers. If Scripture reveals God and what is important to him, then this subject is high on his scale of priorities. If we are concerned to be biblical Christians, the union and unity of believers must come high on our list, too.

Union and unity, however, are not the same. By *union* I mean the basic spiritual relationship which exists among believers regardless of the kind of experience they have of it. By *unity* I mean the experience of union. In other words, the union of Christians exists even when they are angry, divided, antagonistic or hurtful toward each other. But unity in such circumstances is seriously damaged. Union does not need to be created; unity, however, needs continual attention. The Bible teaches much about both aspects, though union is primarily a new covenant idea.

Unity in the Old Testament
"How good and pleasant it is when brothers live together in unity!" This opening to Psalm 133 shows that unity is indeed a significant thought in the Old Testament. From the beginning God thought it "not good" for a man to be alone (Gen 2:18). He made a companion for Adam, a person who "corresponded" to him. God intended that we be social creatures, complementing and interacting with each other, even while we interact with God. Imagine what might have happened in this world *socially*, if sin and the devil had not intruded.

Within the old covenant community God provided a small oasis of brotherhood and unity. Under Moses, careful plans were adopted by which God's people were protected from loss and harsh treatment (see Lev 25:25-55). Debts between Israelites were to be forgiven in the seventh year (Deut 15:1-2). Loans were to be without interest between brother Israelites (Deut 23:19-20). Widows, orphans and children were to be given special attention by the community. God's people were to take great care to remain separate from their noncovenant neighbors, in part so as to maintain their own unity. Some of this became part of Israel's culture, but the record of the Old Testament does not describe outstanding success. The prophets called God's people again and again to return to social righteousness and the unity of God's community.

New Covenant Unity

It grieves thoughtful Christians that unity among new covenant believers is often an elusive dream. The wreckage of God's social plans for us, even in the Christian community, is still evident. I remember well an incident which occurred many years ago, when one prominent evangelical wrote to another, who was in the beginning stages of an important campaign. In his letter, which was highly critical of the second evangelist's strategy, the writer said, "I am praying that if it please God he might strike you dead and thereby stop the harm that you are doing." Such angry divisions among Christian leaders exist today as well.

The grief such divisions produce becomes especially sharp when we think of what the new covenant makes possible. No new covenant privilege needs to be sounded with greater urgency. Unity is at the very heart of the gospel mystery.

The New Testament issues this call in exceptionally strong terms: "Make every effort to keep the unity of the Spirit through the bond of peace" (Eph 4:3 NIV). "I appeal to you, brothers, in the name of our Lord Jesus Christ, that all of you agree with one another so that there may be no divisions among you and that you may be perfectly united in mind and thought" (1 Cor 1:10 NIV). "May the God who gives endurance and encouragement give you a spirit of unity among yourselves as you follow Jesus Christ, so that with one heart and mouth you may glorify the God and Father of our Lord Jesus Christ" (Rom 15:5-6 NIV). "Finally, all of you, live in harmony with one another; be sympathetic, love as brothers, be compassionate and humble" (1 Pet 3:8 NIV).

Consider the astonishing teaching of Ephesians 2:11-22 about the redemptive work of Christ. While many of the passages describing Christ's redemptive work deal with individual salvation, this passage speaks about how he redeemed us from division and hostility. Talking about Jews and Gentiles, Paul says that Christ "Himself is our peace, who made both groups into one, and broke down the barrier of the dividing wall, by abolishing in His flesh the enmity . . . that in Himself He might make the two into one new man, thus establishing peace, and might reconcile them both in one body to God through the cross, by it having put to death the enmity" (2:14-16 NASB).

This is a remarkable view of the cross. Not only were individual offenses that divide from God atoned for, so that we are reconciled with him, but human divisions and antagonisms were slain in his death, so that we are reconciled with one another in Christ. To recall the expression from Romans 7, this too is provided for us "by the dead body of Christ," that is, by his crucifixion. Paul also emphasizes the creation of a new humanity in which former enemies are at peace with each other. This is a major accomplishment of Christ's death and resurrection; it has been completed and results secured in Christ's person.

Ephesians 2 ends with the strong new covenant emphasis on the union established among parts of Christ's body by the indwelling of the Holy Spirit: "In him the whole building is joined together and rises to become a holy temple in the Lord. And in him you too are being built together to become a dwelling in which God lives by his Spirit" (2:21-22 NIV).

The union of believers *exists* already. It does not need to be created; it *has been created* in Christ. Every true believer in Christ is indwelt by the same Holy Spirit of God and so is joined, not only in a real union with Christ, but in a real union with every other Christian. Every time we divide from another Christian, even with cause, it must grieve the Holy Spirit who indwells both of us. Union is always present and real—just as real as the Holy Spirit himself. It does not need to be created, but it does need to be demonstrated.

The reality of Christ's accomplishments, the reality of his exalted state as Head of his body the church, the reality of a new shared relationship with the Holy Spirit—these are part of the new covenant revelation which radically alters our view of each other. A new and higher level of working unity is available to Christians.

Growing in Unity

How are we going to grow in unity? Although much responsibility rests on us, we can be encouraged, knowing that Jesus has already dealt victoriously with all our divisions, and even with the things that cause divisions. He has already established a real union and covenant fellowship of believers. As reflected in his "high priestly" prayer for unity in John 17, he prays constantly that we may experience that unity. But again we must echo his prayers and live accordingly before we can grow in unity. How to proceed may perplex us, and I certainly don't want to sound as though I am trying to give easy and pat answers. Yet the very nature of new covenant truth surely sets some guidelines within which we can make progress. There is reason for hope, in spite of our poor experiences in the past.

Much of our progress in Christian unity will take place through our individual growth in Christian graces. The principles of life discussed in chapter seven on victory must be applied to those areas of our sinful nature that tend to promote division. We *can* make progress in overcoming anger, resentment, jealousy, fear, partisanship, indifference, self-centeredness and pride. We *can* develop a better self-image, more internal peace, patience and endurance, more freedom from guilt. We can become more alert to the enemy's attempts to act as a deceiver and accuser and more successful in resisting him. We have much going for us: the victory of Christ, his intercession for us, our union with him, the presence of his Spirit to give us power. With these resources we can walk in such fellowship with Christ that his attitudes begin to be formed in us: his love, his unconditional acceptance of his people, his servant heart, his real caring for the welfare of others in his body, his genuine delight in his own. There really is no other way. It is tempting to think that there is some "how to" formula that will quickly produce the unity we want, but this deep-level growth in Christ is what we really must have.

When I was a very young minister, I was for a time closely associated with another minister of my own age. In fact, our two families shared living quarters. We were eager, zealous, a bit rambunctious and involved in the excitement of starting a new inner-city work. We could be quite cutting in our remarks about those with whom we disagreed, and frequently we discussed the politics of Christ's kingdom with vigor and not much charity.

And then my friend's father-in-law arrived for a visit. He was a marvelous, godly old servant of Christ, a retired missionary, who delighted us by seeming quite willing to learn new things from us young fellows, participating eagerly in our conversations. But by and by we began to notice an interesting impact he was having on us. When we began to speak critically of other Christians, we became aware that he just stopped talking. He simply would not participate in the conversation as long as we were doing that. He didn't take us to task. He just waited silently. Somehow, we began to lose our zeal to pursue our verbal butchering, the conversation would grind to a halt, and we actually came under the Holy Spirit's conviction for our unloving attitudes. Out of the old man's kindly silence flowed a powerful influence toward unity in Christ's body.

If we advance in these attributes, our experience of unity will less and less depend on others "treating us right." Forgiveness, the soft answer that turns away wrath, moving toward people instead of away when division threatens, acceptance that is not built on performance, genuine delight in each other, the appreciation of each others' gifts—these are things that make us peacemakers, even when others are acting in terribly divisive ways. There is no short cut to this.

Truth and Unity

Many Christians make truth the essential test of unity. Yet our union in Christ goes far deeper than a unified understanding of *all* truth. You and I may not agree on whether handbells should be played in the Sunday morning worship service, yet still be indwelt by the same Holy Spirit. Let's be more realistic. Two Christians may not agree about whether tongues-speaking is legitimate for our day according to Scripture, yet still be joined in Jesus Christ.

On the other hand, we cannot throw away all the gospel and still produce genuine Christians. There is an irreducible minimum of truth that brings a person to faith and incorporates him into the body of Christ. Without it there is no union and there is no body. Scriptures that define the "good news" and the content of saving faith must be taken seriously. Without attempting to be totally precise at this point, I would say that the death and resurrection of Christ (1 Cor 15:1-4), faith as a commitment to Christ as Savior and Lord (Rom 10:9-10), and some level of repentance for sin (Lk 13:3, 5) would seem to be parts of that irreducible minimum. Even so, we have to allow for some measure of uncertainty from our human perspective as to whether or not these factors have been effective in a given person's life. Jesus made it clear that a new birth must take place if a person is to enter heaven, but new life is not always easy to recognize.

At any rate, we should recognize the principle that there is a basic gospel which God uses to make Christians, and then acknowledge that true union in Christ exists among us, even without additional conformity of understandings.

Nonetheless, you and I need to pursue unity with other Christians in all biblical truth. Truth that is not essential to salvation is still important truth. If the role of Scripture is to build fellowship with God, the neglect of any part of it is a significant loss. However, in seeking unity of understanding on secondary levels of truth, we must learn to proceed without making conformity a test of basic acceptance. We may legitimately decide that we can form ourselves into functioning units better when we have conformity on some of these issues, whether it be handbells or tongues-speaking, modes of baptism, or forms of church government. But our basic acceptance of each other as Christians ought not to be at issue.

In learning to work with others toward unity in truth, we have great assets in the Christian community. The Word itself and the

Spirit of truth give great promise of success. The search will of necessity involve discerning our cultural biases, appreciating the unique slants that other minds can give, and much faith, patience and love. Open, listening dialog is a powerful aid.

A Pattern for Unity

Responsibility rests on all of us to heed the New Testament calls and to work toward more unity. Before we take outward steps and during every phase of our endeavor we must seek inward personal growth and prevailing activity in prayer. In this we seek to become agents Christ can use for peacemaking.

Beyond this are positive actions for unity-seekers to take. The following pattern covers some of the major items.

Take personal actions of faith. Decide that you will operate on the realities of the new covenant that we have studied. This is more than saying, "Well, it sounds good; I think it is probably true." It is rather a choice of the will: "If these things are really so, if Christ has already conquered division, if I share his Spirit with all true believers, if union is a fact, then I will operate on this reality.

Decide that you will choose to accept the other members of the body of Christ unconditionally—the same way Christ has accepted both you and them. Philip Henry wrote a baptismal covenant for his children which included the statement: "I take God's people to be my people in every condition." This is the sort of action I am talking about. It is especially important to take this action of faith when you are in the middle of a divisive scene yourself.

Decide that you will commit yourself to the welfare of other Christians. Paul said, "We do not preach ourselves, but Jesus Christ as Lord, and ourselves as your servants for Jesus' sake." And again, "Though I am free and belong to no man, I make myself a slave to everyone" (2 Cor 4:5 and 1 Cor 9:19 NIV). The servant heart comes from Jesus himself and the Holy Spirit can give it to you. But you must make the decisive choice.

Decide that you will unconditionally forgive. One kind of forgiveness the New Testament talks about is the kind you give when a person asks you for it. But Paul talks about a different kind of forgiveness when he says "forgiving each other, just as in Christ God forgave you" (Eph 4:32 NIV). The word here contains the idea of "extending grace" to someone. It is a matter of unmerited favor, the same kind we receive when Christ forgives us.

Do things together that unite. Study the Scriptures with other Christians. Pray together, worship and praise together, find ways to share your lives together. Pool your gifts for ministry projects with other Christians. You will have actual experiences of knowing the presence of the Holy Spirit together in these activities, and your unity will grow.

Study the New Testament concept of mutual encouragement (see 2 Cor 1 and Heb 3:13-14) and become an encourager.

Work toward unity in truth. Assuming that the irreducible core of truth that brings salvation is present on both sides of a difference of opinion, our acceptance of each other is not at stake in such discussions. Approach the Scriptures prayerfully and with confidence in the teaching skill of the Holy Spirit. Do a lot of listening and be ready to grow in your own understanding. Often the uniting truth is larger than either side knew when the discussions started.

Apply the same principles to larger group relationships. Groups can sin as groups and need to repent and confess these sins. Groups can honor the Spirit of Christ and grow in grace. Somehow we also must find ways to approach each other over the boundaries of secondary denominational differences and interact with Jesus' people in other places.

New covenant reality *mandates* our progress toward greater unity. It is right at the heart of the mystery that was previously concealed, but now has been revealed for twenty centuries! We mock the Savior's accomplishments when we divide.

In the four chapters of part two, we have explored the nature of new covenant living—in prayer, victory, guidance and unity. These serve to show something of the comprehensive wonder of life in Christ. In the next section we will look at some of the ways in which we fall short of a new covenant lifestyle, noting some of the chief roadblocks that keep us from making progress in spiritual dynamics.

PART III

ROADBLOCKS TO SPIRITUAL PRIVILEGES

CHAPTER 10

AN INCOMPLETE MESSAGE

---

*A*s I was thinking about the subject of this chapter, I got to daydreaming about an excursion to our favorite restaurant. We had been saving our money to go out to eat. There was a restaurant in town that we liked very much, and we had been hearing reports that it had a new set of entrees on its menu. The word was getting around that it was really outstanding, so we were eager to try it. Finally the day came. We were quite excited to be back at the old eating place. It had a beautiful decor and atmosphere, items that mean a lot to Joyce. As we were led to our table, we peeked at what some of the other diners were eating, and sure enough, a lot looked different from anything we had seen there before.

The waiter was new to us, but seemed very intent on pleasing. He brought us our menus, and we began to search for the great new culinary masterpieces. To our surprise and disappointment, all of the offerings were quite familiar. The prices had gone up since the last time we were there, and maybe there was a new frill here and there or a new description of a meal, but search as we would, we could not find any new dishes at all. We finally ordered a couple of our favorite selections and had a good time anyway. But we couldn't help wondering where all those reports of new things had originated.

Later we made an interesting discovery. Somehow our new waiter had discovered a drawerful of old menus. Thinking that they were the ones in use, he had been handing them out instead of the new ones. He was a fine, cheerful waiter and gave us wonderful attention, but we didn't get any of the new food.

Those who serve at the gospel feast are of course supposed to bring us the full menu of the house. But many of them apparently do not know about the new covenant menu. By failing to bring the new menu they are effectively keeping the Christian diners from partaking of the new feast. This is probably the most appalling tragedy of the church today.

Perhaps this seems like an overstatement. But remember the significance of the new covenant message. It brings to light privileges unknown in old covenant times. As a *covenant* message, it deals with the greatest blessing we human beings can have: fellowship with our God. As a *new* covenant message, it presents the victorious and exalted Christ and a new level of intimacy with his Spirit. And as *the Word of God* it has the power in God's hands to establish and develop that fellowship in all its elevated power and joy. Whether we are looking at preaching, teaching or counseling, the absence of new covenant insights is a devastating roadblock to our experience of our new covenant spiritual privileges. Regrettably, there is a great famine of new covenant insights in gospel communications today. Bits and pieces are present, but seldom a knowledgeable handling of these truths.

For the sake of clarity, let me summarize what I see as the essential features of the new covenant message:

1. The full view of what Christ accomplished by his death and resurrection in handling the human problem.

2. His present glory, exalted power and living reality.

3. His present effective intercession and claim as our Head and covenant-keeper.

4. The gift of the Holy Spirit in a new depth of personal and corporate indwelling.

5. Our real and vital union with Christ, brought about by the presence of the Holy Spirit.

6. Our real and vital union with all other Christians by the shared presence of the Holy Spirit.

7. The significance of our connection with both the old life and the new and the means of dealing effectively with the conflict between flesh and Spirit.

8. The reality of conflict with Satan and the way our union with Christ gives us the tools for exercising authority over him.

9. The biblical faith-responses by which we grow in new covenant glory and power, both individually and with others.

Preaching and Teaching

If you move around within the evangelical community, you will find at least three levels of preaching and teaching that claim to be biblical, but are incomplete from a new covenant standpoint.

An overemphasis on old covenant atmosphere. While paying some attention to Christ, some evangelical preachers seem to make acceptance with God depend on our performance of his demands. One form of this features a strong emphasis on prohibitions regarding amusements, entertainment, diet or clothing. It is not so much the presence of such standards that puts them in this category, but the implication, spoken or unspoken, that our acceptance by God depends on our performance in these matters. In some areas of the church, so much emphasis is placed on the continuity of Old and New Testaments that little place is found for new covenant teachings, and the old seem to predominate. When the Old Testament is preached or taught in this way, there is not a sense of movement from Old Testament to New Testament. There are even some surprising voices in the church today which advocate going back to the Mosaic Law with its harsh punishments such as death for adultery, and a theocratic government, if that could be achieved.

Evangelical nongospel communication. You will be surprised, if you listen carefully, at how often even the skeleton of the gospel is missing from otherwise biblical, evangelical communications. For example, you may hear a sermon which contains an impassioned appeal to "accept Christ as personal Savior," extolling his virtues and eloquently presenting the human need that he will satisfy. It sounds great, until you suddenly realize that the speaker did not mention either the atonement of Christ or his resurrection—the center of the good news that we Christians have to give. Look at your evangelistic tracts. They sometimes omit these points, too. In such instances people are being urged to go through a door that has not been opened.

During my college days I went with teams of students who served as counselors at weekly evangelistic rallies in a nearby city. Leading evangelical preachers of the day spoke at these rallies, and 2000 or more people attended each one. I remember eight consecutive weeks when the fact that Jesus Christ had died for our sins and risen from the grave was not mentioned. These were "gospel preachers." Many passionate appeals were made for response to Christ, but not even a minimal gospel was present.

Skeletal gospel communication. This is by far the most frequent kind of preaching and teaching in evangelical circles. I am thankful that many are careful to put the basic gospel into their preaching and teaching. We can expect the Holy Spirit to bring positive results from this kind of preaching. But tragically, even among these communicators we rarely hear new covenant themes proclaimed.

The Old Testament prophesied the basic outline of what the Messiah would accomplish. As we have seen earlier, Jesus explained these things to his disciples after his resurrection, since they had been blind to them earlier. They learned that the Messiah was to die and rise again from the dead, and that forgiveness should be preached in his name to all nations. This message can be preached without the New Testament Scriptures at all. In fact, this is precisely what the apostles did at first. They, of course, knew about Christ's life and teachings, and this was part of their message.

What they did not have at first was the further revelation that Christ promised to give them and which we have been discussing in this book. They did not have the "mystery" that had been hidden from previous generations, around which the New Testament Scriptures began to be formed. While these new understandings did not displace the skeletal gospel of atonement/resurrection/forgiveness, they did fill it out and inaugurate a new set of spiritual privileges beyond the old covenant possibilities. This is obviously important for God's people to hear.

Omitting or obscuring new covenant truths closes the door to the life that should grow out of them. Many Christians, perhaps you among them, sit under strong preachers who proclaim in a deeply convicting way that the Christian faith ought to result in love, forgiveness, witness and holiness. But they do not tell how grace now operates to produce these virtues. They do not tell about the Comforter and the way he works to bring these things into experience. The essential dynamics for new covenant living are absent. The result of this is to lay on us a burden of "ought" without telling us "how." The skeletal gospel comes in when the preacher tells you that if you fail to meet the "ought" there will be an open door for confession and forgiveness because of what Christ has done. Overall you learn what your life ought to be like and what to do when you fail, but not how Christ and his Spirit can work to transform your life. This is not a new covenant message, and it will be frustrating over the long run.

Think about prayer, for example. You may well have heard strong calls to prayer from the passages of Scripture that encourage Christians to do it, examples from Paul's prayer life or the prayer life of our Lord ("If he needed to pray, you surely must!"), cautions about the wrong kinds of praying, encouragement to pray for the work of the gospel. But have you heard anything about the privileges that are yours in union with the interceding Christ, about the way the Holy Spirit intercedes within you and reflects Christ's praying in your mind, about the way the Holy Spirit unites you with other Christians in prayer? Have you heard about this new covenant level of prayer that is different and more powerful than anything before?

Or what about personal victory over sin? You may well have heard sermons that described different kinds of sins: an unforgiving spirit, pride, self-centeredness, gossip, materialism, failure to care for the needy, and sexual sins. You have probably heard calls to repentance and confession, to "get right with God so that his blessing can be on your life." You have heard about the dangers of backsliding. But have you had the significance of your union with Christ in his dying to sin explained to you? Have you been told about the civil war inside you between the Holy Spirit and your old nature and how the Holy Spirit can help you by applying to your life the power of Christ's victory over sin?

Because some churches know only the bare bones of the atonement/resurrection/forgiveness skeleton, without new covenant concepts, they may develop a rationale for their existence which is solely evangelistic. They think they exist just to make new Christians. The most that is urged upon Christians is repentance and confession—always backward looks. Christian growth is seen almost exclusively in terms of staying active in witnessing. As a result many Christians who are extremely active in the church's outward ministry may become practical skeptics about their personal problems.

Christian Counseling

Christian counseling sometimes bears little relationship to the gospel and can easily become professional, secular counseling done by Christians. Most people expect something more than that when the term Christian counseling is used. They expect it to be in some degree another opportunity for the church to give its message, now however in a much more personal and skillful way, usually one on one, or one on two, and with personal problems directly addressed. The need for this ministry seems to have enlarged tremendously in recent years.

New covenant understandings are crucially important to Christian counseling. They center around the fundamental fact that human beings were created for fellowship with God—a genuine mind-to-mind, feelings-to-feelings, will-to-will interaction of whole persons. In the broadest and deepest sense, we are not basically *healthy* unless we are functioning in this fellowship. Sin is not only deeds that transgress God's law, but the basic drive toward independency and rebellion that has become deeply ingrained in human nature. The cross of Christ is not only an atonement by which we obtain forgiveness and acquittal from God's judgment, but also a reconciliation to God.

With regard to reconciliation the old order indeed included atonement, resurrection and a message of forgiveness. The new covenant, however, centers on a Christ who is triumphant and gloriously contemporary, on a real union with him and on a new level of intimacy with the indwelling Holy Spirit of God. Now as never before the gospel holds out to us an effective way of dealing with the independency of our sinful nature and a walk in the fullness of the Holy Spirit. In other words, it holds out health.

The same basic dynamics are at work in our relationships with other people. Harmony with other persons is best built on mutual fellowship with God. The blight of independency, which so hurts our fellowship with God, hurts our relationships with others too. We "protect our turf" out of fear, envy, jealousy and desire. We exploit each other, degrade each other, are indifferent and unloving toward each other, even while we suffer from loneliness, insecurity and the longing to be understood, loved and needed. By exposing and dealing directly with the personal causes of friction and promoting fellowship with God, new covenant dynamics are the central answer to human relational problems.

If these things are true about new covenant dynamics, Christian counseling cannot afford to ignore them. This does not mean that gospel counseling and the insights of careful psychological research are mutually exclusive. A gospel that exalts the ministry of the Holy Spirit never needs to fear truth, from whatever source it comes. What is needed is an integration of psychological insights with the essential gospel by sensitive Christian counselors, who never lose sight of the central source of personality health.

In a church scene that is superficial in its understanding of the new covenant, Christian counseling often shows the same lack. Sometimes it centers on a kind of old covenant orientation, where freedom from guilt is assumed to be the essence of health. Other times it may emphasize other facets of truth. Sometimes the use of these insights may produce dramatic results. In the long run, however, a person benefiting from such therapy, and consequently much more in touch with himself, may still be using his larger freedom for personal aims only. He has failed to achieve the more basic health of increased fellowship with God.

Professional Christian counselors, observing the superficial results of much "gospel" counseling, and not understanding the true heart of new covenant hope themselves, may see no use for a biblical gospel at all for the more serious cases of need. Rather, they swing over to "scientific" methods of psychology. They deplore and resent attempts of all nonprofessionals to minister to anything but the simplest kinds of "normal" needs. This in turn divides the pastoral community into two groups: those who become enamored of that reasoning and bow to it, and those who feel that this is an attack on the efficacy of the gospel and become antagonistic to all professional help. Meanwhile people continue to cry for help. A new day for Christian counseling will dawn, when a full-orbed gospel uses all legitimate sources of truth and helps troubled people walk with God.

I do not want to throw stones at today's communicators of the gospel. I have again and again been blessed by the faithful commitment and earnest devotion of many. I know that many love the Savior every bit as much as I do. I am a Christian because of a faithful preacher whom the Lord used to touch my soul. I am not implying a lack of commitment, but a lack of message. And I am truly alarmed by the practical skepticism I see among God's people—people who have come to believe that there really is little help for them in their Christian faith. Their personal problems, their marital difficulties, their hassles with their children are deeply perplexing, but many have resigned themselves to frustration. In the light of what Christ has done and who he is, in the light of our union with him and the intimate presence of the powerful Holy Spirit, this ought not to be!

CHAPTER 11

MATERIALISM

O *ne day I passed the TV set at home where I noticed an evangelist preach-ing.* Something he said caught my attention, and I stopped to listen for five minutes. "God wants your happiness," he was saying, "your prosperity, your success. Jesus became poor in order that you might become rich. If you do not enjoy material success, something is wrong with your faith, for that is part of your redemption bless-ings." He put into his remarks a large number of Scripture texts to support his case, and his well-dressed, middle-class audience enthu-siastically applauded his message.

Some parts of the evangelical church rather scornfully call preachers of this sort the "health and wealth boys," and suggest that they ought to be sent to Haiti or Ethiopia to see how their message would go over in the poverty-stricken areas of the world. But scorn does not really serve to answer the evangelist's message. There are indeed some strong Scriptures used in support of such ideas.

As I stood there watching, it suddenly occurred to me that the chief difficulty of this man's message was that it was basically an old covenant idea and did not adequately take into account some of the changes brought about by our great covenant-keeper Jesus. More than that, he was urging his audience to focus on things of the old covenant period that were designed to be mere shadows of the riches that were coming in Christ. To seek these as goals of our redemption now is like preferring junk food to the real thing. Let us examine the difference between the two eras in regard to possessions.

Old Covenant Prosperity

Right from the time of God's covenant dealings with Abraham, a land of promise was prominent: "To your offspring [seed] I will give this land" (Gen 12:7 NIV, see also 13:14; 15:18; 17:7-8). There was both a material and long-range aspect to this promise. The material fulfillment came about when Moses and Joshua led the Israelites into Canaan, fought physical enemies, apportioned homesteads and began to eat the fruit of the land. The Genesis 17 reference, on the other hand, speaks of the covenant as an "everlasting covenant" and the land as "an everlasting possession." This, together with the term *seed*, which according to Galatians has its final focus in Christ himself (Gal 3:16), opens up a dual fulfillment of the land promise. In view from Abraham's time on is a later Messianic fulfillment, as well as a more immediate promise.

The old covenant under Moses strongly emphasized the physical blessings which would be associated with careful keeping of the Law. "If you follow my decrees and are careful to obey my commands, I will send you rain in its season, and the ground will yield its crops. . . . You will eat all the food you want and live in safety in your land. . . . You will pursue your enemies, and they will fall by the sword before you" (Lev 26:3-7 NIV). Just at the point of entering the promised land, God said to Joshua, "I will give you every place where you set your foot. . . . Do not let this Book of the Law depart from your mouth; meditate on it day and night, so that you may be careful to do everything written in it. *Then you will be prosperous and successful*" (Josh 1:3, 8 NIV, italics added).

Tithing material blessings was part of covenant responsibility. This material outlook is still in place in the last book of the Old Testament, where God says, "Bring the whole tithe into the storehouse. . . . Test me in this, . . . and see if I will not throw open the floodgates of heaven and pour out so much blessing that you will not have room for it. . . . Then all the nations will call you blessed, for yours will be a delightful land" (Mal 3:10, 12 NIV).

The ultimate picture of covenant blessing in Mosaic times was materially prosperous people living in a land which was the place of God's dwelling with his people—every man under his own vine and fig tree, enjoying the early and latter rains and good crops, living on the ancestral homestead with its boundaries kept carefully intact. All of this could be lost if the covenant obligations were broken.

But before the material blessings of the land were lost, the temple destroyed and the people removed from their homeland, the promise came to a climax in the kingdom under David and Solomon. The land reached its largest extent. Enemies were subjugated on all sides. One of the most beautiful temples of all history was built for God's habitation with his people. Riches abounded and surrounding nations marveled. The Promised Land, under the old covenant, reached its high point.

Shadow vs. Substance

Hebrews 11 makes plain that the people of faith under the old covenant saw something beyond the material signs of their day: "They were longing for a better country—a heavenly one. Therefore God is not ashamed to be called their God, for he has prepared a city for them" (Heb 11:16 NIV).

This is consistent with what we have seen already. The old covenant believer saw by the prophets a coming era that would have greater glory than anything yet seen. We recognize this at once in things that Jesus said. "I came that they might have life, and might have it abundantly" (Jn 10:10 NASB).

Ah! The abundant life! We Americans know that expression, don't we? Jesus told parables about the kingdom of heaven being like a treasure hidden in a field that a man gives up all his previous possessions to obtain, or a pearl of great value that a merchant buys at great cost (Mt 13:44-46). Clearly the riches of the new era far exceed those of the old.

Then remember statements like these: "He who did not spare his own Son, but gave him up for us all—how will he not also, along with him, graciously give us all things?" (Rom 8:32 NIV). God is described as the One "who richly provides us with everything for our enjoyment" (1 Tim 6:17 NIV). And perhaps most staggering of all are these words of Paul: "All things are yours, whether Paul or Apollos or Cephas or the world or life or death or the present or the future—all are yours, and you are of Christ, and Christ is of God" (1 Cor 3:21-23 NIV). This is staggering! The world belongs to you! And life! The present belongs to you! Here are riches unimaginable—all yours as a Christian. The outlook of the new covenant is that of *real* wealth, something that the old was merely pointing toward.

But let's look at these new riches more closely. Before we decide that we are entitled to drive around in a Cadillac, although King Solomon only had a Model T, other sounds in the New Testament have to be heard. Jesus, for example, also said, "Lay not up for yourselves treasures upon earth, where moth and rust doth corrupt, and where thieves break through and steal: But lay up for yourselves treasures in heaven. . . . For where your treasure is, there will your heart be also" (Mt 6:19-21 KJV). He spoke of how hard it is for a rich man to enter heaven (Lk 18:24-25). He said things like: "Any of you who does not give up everything he has cannot be my disciple" (Lk 14:33 NIV). In Christ's way of operating we die in order to live; new life abundance does not necessarily mean material possessions. "Watch out!" Jesus said, "Be on your guard against all kinds of greed; a man's life does not consist in the abundance of his possessions" (Lk 12:15 NIV).

Paul echoes Jesus, and just as strongly. He talks about "Men of corrupt mind, who have been robbed of the truth and who think that godliness is a means to financial gain. . . . People who want to get rich fall into temptation and a trap and into many foolish and harmful desires that plunge men into ruin and destruction. For the love of money is a root of all kinds of evil. Some people, eager for money, have wandered from the faith and pierced themselves with many griefs" (1 Tim 6:5, 9-10 NIV). Paul here goes on to tell Christians who do have money how to act, that they should "do good, . . be rich in good deeds, and . . . be generous and willing to share. In this way they will lay up treasure for themselves as a firm foundation for the coming age, so that they may take hold of the life that is truly life" (6:18-19 NIV).

New Covenant Prosperity

Riches in Christ, then, do not necessarily include material prosperity, riches for personal, private enjoyment. Hebrews describes the difference in these words, when the writer speaks to those who "joyfully accepted the confiscation of your property, because you knew that you yourselves had better and lasting possessions" (Heb 10:34 NIV). New covenant possessions are *better* than the old style prosperity that foreshadowed them. Paul said it this way: "I have learned to be content in whatever circumstances I am. I know how to get along with humble means, and I also know how to live in prosperity; in any and every circumstance I have learned the secret of being filled and going hungry, both of having abundance and suffering need. I can do all things through Him who strengthens me" (Phil 4:11-13 NASB). Paul would have been astounded at the idea that his times of material want came about because of lack of faith!

How then should we understand new covenant prosperity? What we find under the new covenant is first of all and paramountly *Christ himself*. But what a Christ! King of kings and Lord of lords! Beginning of a new creation that is supplanting the old! Triumphant over the world, the flesh and the devil! We are now joined to him and have become the temple of his Holy Spirit. In Christ there is a new creation; old things have passed away and all things have become new. This is the reality of which the old covenant contained but preliminary shadows. Because he has conquered all, in him everything belongs to us: the world, the present, the future, life, death, *everything* is ours, as Paul said. But it is ours only in union with Christ, and that union is also a union with him in death to our own way, our own selfish pleasures, our independent self-gratification. We are now kingdom persons under David's greater Son, involved in the greatest kingdom-establishing enterprise that ever has been.

Of course the King will watch over his own. Of course he wants our happiness and satisfaction. But whatever comes through our hands now is for his purposes and his enterprise. Our joy and fulfillment will come as we live in harmony with the One to whom we are joined. "Seek first his kingdom and his righteousness, and all these things will be given to you as well" (Mt 6:33 NIV). "No one who has left home or brothers or sisters or mother or father or children or fields for me and the gospel will fail to receive a hundred times as much in this present age (homes, brothers, sisters, mothers, children and fields—and with them, persecutions) and in the age to come, eternal life" (Mk 10: 29-30 NIV).

At any time or period of our life, the Lord may call on us to go through suffering or deprivation for his sake and the gospel's. Perhaps some are called to live in the midst of abject poverty in order to carry out kingdom purposes. Others, for the sake of the kingdom, may have goods poured through their hands. The message of the new covenant is that we are unconquerably rich in every condition of this life. We have better and enduring possessions that this world cannot take away. In any case, the Lord has absolute claim on every part of our lives and possessions. We are his stewards at all times. This is a rich condition; to seek this world's goods for ourselves is to be poverty-stricken in comparison, a decline from the new covenant abundance and a roadblock to its fulfillment.

Other Forms of Materialism

We are rich in Christ by virtue of our union with him. Our riches are *spiritual* in the sense that they come to us through the Holy Spirit. Christ has dominion over the world and the entire material realm, so we will share his triumph there, too, regardless of the economics he chooses for our lives. But the Holy Spirit also radically raises our consciousness concerning spiritual dimensions of life. To fail to operate in these realms is another form of material orientation and a falling away from the new covenant privileges.

An example of this is the new outlook we should have on conflict. Under the old covenant, with its physical setting, enemies were physical enemies and were dealt with in a decidedly physical way. Almost instinctively we recognize a change when we read the Old Testament now. We study the battle campaigns and strategies of Joshua and make application to our own conflicts in a spiritualized way. We pass over with hardly a thought that for them this war was a daily bloodbath, which meant putting to the sword women and children as well as enemy soldiers.

This physical orientation no doubt led to certain mindsets. Retribution and revenge were common attitudes, very physically expressed. Hatred of enemies was assumed and taught. Take the beautiful "Waters of Babylon" Psalm, for example. It ends "Happy is he who repays you for what you have done to us—he who seizes your infants and dashes them against the rocks" (Ps 137:8-9 NIV, see also Ps 69:22-28).

Imagine the surprise of John and James in Samaria with Jesus. They had just been on the mountaintop and had had the mind-boggling experience of seeing Christ transfigured and joined by Moses and Elijah. They now come to a Samaritan village filled with people they traditionally despised and are refused hospitality. James and John, the "sons of thunder," ask Jesus if they should call down fire from heaven to burn up the villagers. All versions agree that Jesus rebuked them for this thought (a perfectly natural one for an old covenant believer), and some ancient manuscripts add, "Ye know not what manner of spirit ye are of. For the Son of man is not come to destroy men's lives, but to save them" (Lk 9:55-56 KJV). At any rate, this was of a piece with Jesus' new teaching that they were not to follow the old way of hating their enemies, but to love them and do good to them.

Paul puts the perspective clearly: "Put on the full armor of God, that you may be able to stand firm against the schemes of the devil. For our struggle is not against flesh and blood, but against the rulers, against the powers, against the world forces of this dark-

ness, against the spiritual forces of wickedness in the heavenly places" (Eph 6:11-12 NASB). Where the old covenant believer had
almost no instruction about warfare against spiritual powers of
darkness, the new covenant believer is told that this is where the
conflict really centers. We do not need to waste energy fighting
against other human beings. By the Spirit's help, we can go directly
to the heart of the conflict in the spiritual realm and approach our
human enemies with grace and forgiveness.

It takes supernatural grace from the Holy Spirit to live this way,
yet that is precisely what he has come to bring. We are joined to
Christ in his triumph over all spiritual foes, and now are drawn into
the conflict to demonstrate what he has done. Actually it is a great
relief not to have to fight against other human beings. When we
do, we slip back into old covenant materialism.

Perhaps one further illustration is in order, and that is the matter
of tithing. We have noted already that tithing appears in the old
order as a distinctive feature of the covenant community (see Mal
3:7-12). But how does the new covenant affect it? Proportional
giving and the taking of offerings are New Testament principles.
Certainly we as Christians ought not to do less for Christ's kingdom than old covenant believers did in their day.

But all this is beside the point. Commitment that grows out of
union with Christ and the intimate presence of his Spirit in us is
total. The stewardship of life and resources is total, too. Jesus is
King over all our life. Perhaps (and only perhaps) old covenant
believers could pay their tithes and consider the rest of their lives
and possessions their own, to do with as they pleased. But we do
not have that option, whether they did or not. Tithing can be a cop-
out to keep from placing all of life at Christ's disposal. It then
becomes another form of materialism.

It is a narrow door that leads to life, to the truly abundant life
of new covenant riches. Going through it we lose the right to call
anything our own; we have to lay aside all our baggage in order to
get through. But on the other side is the magnificent treasure of
Christ. Once united with him and indwelt by his Spirit, we are
foolish to want to eat the junk food of the old life. To be strangers

and pilgrims, to have no sure dwelling place in this earth, to be wholly at his disposal no matter what his choice is for us, this is unspeakable joy and great privilege. Don't let materialism in any form rob you of your great riches!

CHAPTER 12

LEGALISM

G iven *the failure of our day to explain the new covenant, probably the most* widespread substitute for a new covenant lifestyle is legalism.

I run into many inadequate ideas about legalism, and have partaken of some of them myself. At times when I have been confronted by some regulation or other, I have muttered under my breath, "Legalism again! What right has he to put me under his silly old laws." Or I have heard of some school that puts its students under strict behavior codes and have said, "Boy, I could never study under that kind of legalism. They're worse than Moses!" I have watched the reaction of some young Christians when someone has said quite positively that a Christian "must have a Quiet Time every day or his spiritual life will wither." Their expressions have said quite clearly, "That's mechanical; that's just a form of Christian legalism; I won't buy into that!" I will confess even to a twinge of alarm over Paul's statement that he was "under the law of Christ" (1 Cor 9:21), as though that might be tinged with legalism. I have heard people comment on certain parents who were strict disciplinarians: "Oh, they are way too legalistic with their children."

What Is Legalism?

The mere presence of laws and standards for our Christian living does not in itself indicate legalism. The Bible is full of such standards, New Testament as well as Old. Such standards are definitely important to us. We need to have a clear guide to what God expects of us and accept and desire that level of life. God's impressing these expectations strongly on our consciences and measuring us by them is necessary and important, in fact, a great gift of God to us.

What, then, is legalism? Here is the way I see it: when regulations and standards are imposed and enforced on our behavior, with the aim of producing conformity to them, *legalism places reliance on that process itself to produce the desired results.* The hope is that the very system of imposing and enforcing the law, along with fear of bad consequences for disobedience, will move us to comply with these demands. Such a system may be self-imposed or put on us by an outside authority. In either case, confidence is placed in the regulating system to produce the results.

Scripture makes it plain that this is a misplaced confidence: "For what the law was powerless to do in that it was weakened by the sinful nature, God did by sending his own Son. . . . And so he condemned sin in sinful man, in order that the righteous requirements of the law might be fully met in us, who do not live according to the sinful nature but according to the Spirit" (Rom 8:3-4 NIV). In legalism you are expecting something from your own nature that by itself it cannot give, even though you are a Christian.

How the New Covenant Works

As this important passage from Romans suggests, new covenant living operates by a different set of dynamics. In new covenant living, righteousness has been secured for us in the victorious person of Jesus. It is made available to us through our real union with him, and it is brought about in our experience by the powerful operation of the Holy Spirit. It is activated through a knowledgeable fellowship with the Holy Spirit. He puts us in touch with life and power infinitely greater than our own.

New covenant living does not eliminate either law or discipline, but we put our confidence in the spiritual privileges of our new relationship rather than in the regulatory system itself. We study God's standards in Scripture to know what pleases him. We read the law and are convicted of sin. We want to know and follow God's will. But we expect growth to come through our union with Christ the covenant-keeper and by increased fellowship with his Spirit.

Let me give you an example. Paul says, "Let love be without hypocrisy" (Rom 12:9 NASB). This is a deceptively simple sounding command. Simple or not, we know from it that pure love ought to be the hallmark of our life, especially in the Christian community. But if we do not recognize more than the simple "ought" of this command, we are left in a legalistic bind. In our own nature we do not have pure love. It must come to us from Christ. It is a fruit of the Holy Spirit and is poured out in our hearts by him. As the first verses of Romans 12 tell us, we need an increasing experience of transformation—the "renewing of our minds"—if we are going to experience God's will. Only as we understand union with Christ can we subdue our unloving nature and fellowship with God in his love.

What happens, though, when you are confronted with a fellow Christian whom you naturally dislike, or who has given you much cause to dislike him? First, you might be convicted of your unloving attitude. You *know* that you should love him and that it just won't stand up before God to tell this person that you love him, all the while despising him in your heart. You know your love for him should be genuine, but actually you don't love him at all!

In this kind of situation, we can come to the Holy Spirit with the assurance that he is already moving in the direction we want to go. Jesus has already conquered at the cross our unloving nature, not just so that we can be forgiven, but so that we can find freedom from its weakness. We choose our place of death with Christ. We agree actively to the death of all our rights to be independent in our reactions to our fellow Christian. We invite the Holy Spirit to have fellowship with us in our feelings for our brother. We ask and expect Jesus to share with us his own love for that person. We may have to resist the enemy who is trying to separate us from our brother. Then we move toward the person expectantly.

As true Christian believers we give evidence of a new birth by our deep desire to please God. This desire may at times be somewhat covered over by the rubbish of life, but it is there just the same. The Holy Spirit frequently rekindles it, even at times of backsliding. But the "how"— that sometimes perplexes us.

If we are unaware of or failing to make use of our new covenant privileges, there are not many options left to us. In our struggle to please God we may even become doubtful that Christianity really works. We rightly rely on confession and forgiveness to relieve our consciences regarding failures to reach a higher level, but then sometimes simply have to settle for a lower standard than the Scripture sets. When we are hurting over this, we may not even care to hear the demands of the Law anymore, or at best listen with a dull hopelessness. Usually the only route we know to follow is some form of legalism. We accept the "oughts" of Christianity and strive mightily to achieve them. And we wonder at the small measure of power that seems to be available to us.

When all is said and done, the major reason that legalism is not a viable route to righteousness is that it depends on self-effort. But in our own strength we just don't have what it takes. This is why legalism is so frustrating.

The Appeal of Legalism

While legalism is powerless and frustrating, our sin nature still perversely desires it. Our basic motivation, apart from grace, is toward independence. In spite of all the joys of fellowship with God, we still have to be wary about this. In spite of our desire for the will of God, our flesh often seeks to retrieve some self-respect by trying to carry it out independently. We can even find it worth some misery if we can retain that independence. As the alternative becomes clear—that the way of power is the way of death to self-will and involves a walk in constant fellowship with the sovereign God—our sin nature will writhe and squirm to keep its basic dominance. Legalism, for the very reason that it involves self-effort, is the choice of our flesh.

Now you can see why legalism is one of the chief roadblocks to a new covenant lifestyle. This is so important that I'd like to examine two or three practical areas of experience to see the contrast in each of them between new covenant living and legalism.

Sexuality

As human beings, we have been created with a strong sex drive. This is in itself good, part of God's excellent creation. Part of our human function, our enjoyment of life and the continuance of the race depend on it. But because it is such a strong drive, the struggle to control this area of life and fulfill God's expectations can be severe indeed. On the one hand, as biblically aware Christians, we know that God desires that we control our sexuality. On the other hand, we are surrounded by a world that holds no such standards and flaunts uncontrolled sexuality at us from every side. The teenage years are particularly difficult since peer pressure, a secular school system, the youth culture and new moral permissiveness coincides with a time of mounting strength in the physical drive and considerable immaturity.

How can we achieve control in this area of life? Right here we are hindered by a long history of legalistic approaches. We have probably heard strong teaching and preaching about God's high standards for sex, and the church has generally become much more open about discussing such problems and trying to educate in this sphere. But historically we have expected imposition of the standards and rules to produce the results.

The new covenant way to achieve control begins by recognizing our union with Christ and fellowship with the Holy Spirit in this area of our lives. This may come across to you as strangely diffuse and unsatisfying. The "how to" that you may have been conditioned to expect from typical Christian teaching is a neat package that tells you what to do in various types of situations, unfolds relational psychology and teaches principles of Christian behavior in the sex realm. What is suggested may be true and good, but in themselves they are just another form of legalism. In order to be effective, these must come to us with an underlying foundation of spiritual dynamics, that is, the relationship with Christ that brings his power to bear on our lives. If that is in place, some of these other insights and instructions can be helpful.

These dynamics, as applied to the control of our sexuality, look something like this. Powerful negative forces are at work: our own push toward self-centered, independent operation of our lives (Paul called this "the flesh"); the tempter and his tricks, and the impact of the world. Our emotions and wills, so often deeply involved in our sexual problems, do not function as they were designed to function unless they are operating in fellowship with the Spirit of God. The problem within is not our sex drive itself, but the grab, exploitation and self-gratification that fastens on it when we are not in an accurately established fellowship with God in this area of our lives.

Christ has conquered these very problems at Calvary and possesses the full fruit of this victory in himself as triumphant Lord. Our union with him in death and new life, administered by the Holy Spirit in the specific area of our sexuality, results in a growing fellowship with him right there. This is real and practical and full of power.

The "how to" of a new covenant approach is indicated by the necessity of a prayer-response that echoes Christ's present intercession on our behalf. The power of this relationship is introduced into our actual scene as we make the faith responses that are taught in Scripture, but now specifically focused on the area of our sexuality. Our entire expression of sexuality, our maleness or femaleness, needs to be brought into a living interaction with the Holy Spirit.

Our "flesh" causes a strong push toward independent self-gratification. So right here, on the basis of our union with Christ in his death, we choose our place of death with him, death to our right to independent function and independent gratification of our sexuality. At the same time we invite the Holy Spirit to have fellowship with us in all functions of our sexuality. We should be specific about this, including the ways we project our manhood or womanhood, the ways we react to members of the opposite sex, our expressions of affection, and so on. This is not an attempt to eliminate such projections, reactions or expressions (unless they are obviously wrong), but simply to free our sexuality from autonomy and to invite the Holy Spirit to interact *with* us.

In new covenant living we are free to acknowledge our own legitimate responses as males or females, free to appreciate the beauties and God-designed characteristics of the other sex, but also increasingly free from the grab and exploitation that can mar those expressions and relationships. This kind of living leaves us free to accept God's standards of morality and seek to fulfill them, but by the power of fellowship with the Spirit of God. In this lifestyle there is hope, whereas legalism simply does not work.

Marriage

A lot of debate today surrounds whether marriage is an authority structure. Those who feel that it is usually come down heavy on the headship of the husband and the calls of Scripture for the wife to submit. Those who do not believe that marriage is an authority structure emphasize *egalitarian* marriage, a situation of exact equality of position and role for each partner.

The debate is often confused, however, by the tendency to think legalistically and to be unaware of the new covenant lifestyle. Under the new covenant the authority debate becomes much less critical. I believe that Scripture makes plain that marriage is indeed intended to be an authority structure, that there *is* given to the husband a role of responsible headship in the family under God. Yet apart from functioning within new covenant dynamics, such authority structures can become dangerous and hurtful.

On the other hand, when Christian couples practice new covenant principles in their relationship, there may be little functional difference between those who believe in the authority structure and those who do not. And so the debate becomes much less urgent.

Under legalism we expect the authority structure to bring the results of righteousness. Actually, because of the frailty of human nature, it is powerless to do so. The more vigorous the attempt, the

143

more frustrating the results. The husband is expected to make the decisions and the wife simply to obey them. The wife is encouraged to meet all the demands of the husband, whether or not she feels that they are right and honoring to the Lord. Frequently both parties are under such inward and outward tension that explosions are inevitable.

Under the new covenant, we simply cannot ignore, without severe injury, how we are joined in Christ. We are not only joined to Christ by the Holy Spirit, but we are joined to each other by the same Spirit. We are together submitted to the headship of the living Jesus and are together the temple of his Spirit. We are brothers and sisters as well as husbands and wives, if we are Christians. We have the privilege and responsibility of praying together for the mind of the Lord and supporting each other in doing this. Power struggles are out. When things go wrong with our mate, we have the resource of prevailing prayer and resistance to the enemy, instead of wrestling with flesh and blood. We can draw on Jesus' love, joy, peace, longsuffering, gentleness, goodness and self-control—all powerful instruments of blessing in marriage. Each partner can be watching for ways to support the other with Christ's serving heart, giving room and encouragement for personal growth and development without jealousy or fear. Utopian, you say! Sure it is! We will indeed have to grow toward this, but there is power for it under the new covenant, none under legalism.

Under the new covenant way, we can honor the authority structure without being smothered by it. Husbands can watch over their families as elders in this smallest unit of the church, and be encouraged in this role by their wives. It should never be necessary to stoop to impose law without grace and mutuality.

Raising Children

Caring for small children requires a stronger employment of law. For their own good, we command them not to cross the street or stick scissors in the light socket. We expect training to take place as a consequence of imposing such laws and enforcing them. It's an important process. If you have raised children, you know the perplexity of gradually withdrawing this kind of law-giving as they approach maturity.

However, even when children are small, we need not employ an unsupportive, graceless legalism. Scripture tells us that the family unit is a sanctuary of the Holy Spirit's presence, even when children have not yet made their own commitment to Christ (see 1 Cor 7:13-14). New covenant power can therefore be active in the home derived from joint Bible study, private and family prayer, and an engaging in spiritual conflict against the enemies of the family. There can be mutual leadership under the Holy Spirit by the parents, and prayerful evangelizing under Christ. Love, joy, peace, along with the other fruits of the Spirit, like self-control, create a nurturing atmosphere that is vastly different from legalism.

When children are genuinely committed to Christ by their own choice, new possibilities emerge. There is now something to appeal to in them. Rather than simply laying down the law, we can cover situations in prayer, bind the adversary and approach their seed of desire for the will of God, expecting the Holy Spirit to do his work. We remember that our sons and daughters are now our brothers and sisters in Christ, too, and can be approached that way. Union exists here, even when it seems far from expression. We can encourage our younger brothers and sisters in Christ's way, affirm and appreciate them, watch over their emerging gifts, love them and rejoice over them in Jesus! We can help them learn how to recognize and handle their own flesh, the devil and the world with spiritual weapons. These are things that legalism can never accomplish.

There are no neat packages of rules for raising children, living in marriages, or handling your sexuality. What I am saying is that we are now joined to the King who has won a great victory over every problem that we encounter. His power is brought to us by fellowship with the Holy Spirit, not by systems of rules in themselves. We look at the standards; we study the expectations of God and let God measure our lives by them. But then we seek fellowship with the Holy Spirit in all the specific situations of life. That is the way to grow toward God's goals for our lives.

To some it might seem that what I am advocating is quietism as the proper mode of Christian living: to all problems the answer is just to pray and expect Christ to change us! While it is true that responses to God are generally made by prayer, this would be a gross misunderstanding of the new covenant lifestyle. What is being said is that fellowship with God is the only way we can be whole and healthy and that the new covenant is God's powerful provision for such fellowship to be established. We must start there, and then there may be many sensible and active procedures to follow. Those procedures will be powerless, however, if we are attempting them on our own.

It is easy to come to the Bible with a legalistic expectation. We want it to guide us with a specific rule for every situation where God cares what we do. But that is not the chief function of the Bible. The Bible is the Word of reconciliation, designed to bring us to God and to establish and build our relationship with him. It is *covenant!* It contains law and standards which reveal God's expectations; the Holy Spirit will use these to help us see where we fall short. But fellowship is the goal of the Bible, and in fellowship we find power.

CHAPTER 13

ENCULTURATION

When I was little, I hated to have my mother try out new culinary creations at our family table. Some dishes I knew I liked, and some dishes I knew I didn't like. Anything new I didn't like. "But, Mother, I don't *want* any!" Then would come the quiet but firm reply, "Donald, I want you to try some." And then that unanswerable question, "How can you know that you don't like it until you have tried it?" The fact that it obviously had lumps in it (or peanuts or bones or skins or seeds), that it was too hot or too cold, too gooey or too runny, didn't seem to carry any weight at all. Finally, under the threat of no dessert, I would eat it.

It was the depression years, and our meals couldn't be as varied as perhaps my mother would have liked. So I got used to certain staple foods that I knew I could manage. They were my food world, what I was accustomed to, and I resented intruders. It wasn't really that I didn't trust mother and her cooking. I just liked what I was used to, and that was that.

Enculturation

Sociologists have a fancy word for the process of getting used to something. They call it *enculturation*. The word wasn't even in the dictionary when I was a boy, and the word culture was then defined almost exclusively as a synonym of refinement. There was an implied value dimension to these words. You could be so trained and immersed in the "finer" things of life that they became the habitual expression of your personality. You were then a cultured or refined person.

Today the word culture is often used without any connotation of value. It refers to the whole set of socially transmitted behaviors— whether good or bad—including ethnic traditions, ways of eating (fork tines curved up or down), ways of making music or making love, ways of dressing, speaking, and a thousand other functions. *Enculturation* refers to the process by which these behaviors are transmitted.

The result of this process becomes closely associated with our sense of identity. The feelings we have toward our enculturation and the things that threaten it can easily draw us away from a new covenant walk in fellowship with the Spirit of Jesus.

We cannot avoid being enculturated. Given the kind of beings we are and the kind of minds we have, it is inevitable. In hundreds of ways you and I become conditioned, patterned and traditionalized. If we do things a certain way repeatedly, we become used to that pattern. Then we are most comfortable and secure when we act in the accustomed fashion. Habits are formed and strengthened.

Enculturation, besides being comfortable, often serves constructive purposes. The development of skills and competence is really a form of enculturation, although not often called that. So it is with refinement of taste and discernment, which depend on repeated experiences coupled with value judgments. These kinds of things contribute greatly to our comfort and enjoyment of life. An old, familiar song, performed in a way we have come to consider the height of skill and beauty, brings great satisfaction to us. The same performance to a person without our particular enculturation may be boring. My father used to enjoy getting back to see his beloved sand dunes of Cape Cod, where he had lived as a boy. I would stare at them totally mystified, wondering what on earth he saw in them.

Enculturation makes us vulnerable to much hurt. To some degree we are what we have experienced, or at least we feel that way. Since enculturation is partly produced by the impact of our surroundings on us, when those surroundings change, we go through culture shock. And our surroundings are often changing. Family groupings with which we have lived long and become familiar, suddenly break up, and we feel as though a part of us has been torn away. We are compelled to move from the old homestead, and sights and experiences that have become a part of our very being, it seems, are no longer there. This can hurt a great deal until we gradually adapt to a new scene.

Enculturation and the Gospel
We also receive the gospel in a cultural package. Certain songs are sung repeatedly and in a certain way. Prayers have a form and content that we become used to. A certain form of dress and appearance accompanies worship. The visual scene and arrangement of meeting places are part of our experience and therefore seem a part of us. Old Mrs. Brown in our church couldn't pray if we put the prayer meeting chairs in a circle! Because our faith is an earnest and essential part of our lives, its trappings tend to become important, too. We tend to identify the package the gospel comes in with the gospel itself. If anyone tampers with the package, we feel shock, just as if someone were tampering with the gospel itself. If the young people begin to sing the Scriptures with music that is part of the youth culture (and therefore "not our kind of music"), we may actually suspect them of departing from the faith, without examining their faith at all. And it hurts deeply. It seems as though something is being torn from our vitals, as though our identity as Christians is being threatened. There are few experiences as painful and lonely as culture shock.

We can readily see that this cultural packaging of the gospel, though not wrong in itself, can make our experience of unity with other Christians more difficult. Enculturation can indeed produce a small and rather poor kind of unity—we can enjoy being with Christians of our own kind. But it can have a divisive effect across cultural gaps. The Holy Spirit is not owned by any one form of culture, and it is his shared presence that unites us all in the body of Christ. We can easily become antagonistic to other genuine Christians just because of cultural differences.

There are many other ways that our enculturation can adversely affect our Christian experience. We may become so used to a certain style of preaching or teaching that we actually find it difficult to hear the Spirit's voice unless it comes in that kind of package. Lesson materials or a Christian book may be hard to study if they are not in a style to which we are accustomed.

Enculturation and New Covenant Living

If our enculturation, with its feelings of security or insecurity, keeps us from being open to fresh winds of the Spirit, it has become a deadly enemy of new covenant living. The Lord's plan may be to lead us into paths we have not walked before, to be with people we have not known before and who have different ways and practices. The crucial question then becomes, will we be so dependent for security on our normal cultural patterns that we cannot follow him?

The essence of the gospel is *not* the same as the cultural clothing it wears. We must distinguish the contents of the package from the package itself. The package may enhance the contents. It is inevitable and good that the gospel comes in packages. But the same gospel can and does come in many different packages. It is transcultural. It is more basic and free than its coverings.

Similarly, in Christ our identity is more basic and free than our enculturation. We need to realize this, especially when we suffer from culture shock. We really can adapt to outward changes without losing our identity. Our personal identity does not really depend on our having things the way we are used to having them.

Think of how Christ changed Paul the Jew and Pharisee into a lover and server of Gentiles, even while he continued to value his Jewish heritage. Lots of psychologists would consider such a change impossible because of the depths of enculturation and emotion involved. But that power is there in Jesus, and the Holy Spirit is here to make it real to us. Indeed, until we find the power of Christ to free us from dependence on our enculturation for our security, that very enculturation will block our new covenant fellowship with the Holy Spirit and with other Christians.

I grew up assuming that a theological conservative would also be a political conservative. Of course, when I was little I didn't know anything about such terminology. But I was enculturated, terminology or not. In our little Republican New England town, I cried all the way to school the day after Mr. Roosevelt was elected President of the United States in 1932. I hated him passionately, just as I hated oyster stew, and for no better reasons, certainly not on any rational ground that I had developed for myself. I was in the fourth grade!

The reason we should be theological conservatives is not that we are conservative by nature and feel more comfortable holding doctrines that have always been part of our background. We should be theological conservatives because scriptural truths are what God uses to bring us into fellowship with himself and to build that fellowship. We must not lose any part of that instrument. But if the Scriptures have their intended effect, and we are brought into vital and growing fellowship with the living Christ, we will want to be close to him in whatever he is doing in his kingdom. *He* may not always be interested in maintaining the status quo. Our responsibility is to be right there on the cutting edge of whatever he is doing. Our security is really found in being at his side, not in doing what we are used to.

The danger of a fixed enculturation becomes more acute the older we get. This is natural. We have more and more experience, we become more and more used to certain ways, which tend to become increasingly a part of our security. What is really sad among Christians, or any human beings for that matter, is a state of enculturation with aging that causes people to stop growing. The routines of life so take over that new learning does not take place anymore. We can become less and less open to Christ's leading, if this happens to us.

On the other hand, a close walk with the Lord, in which our security depends on being with him, rather than on doing things in accustomed ways, will tend to keep us flexible and growing through all our days. Earlier in this book I mentioned the impact of an old, retired missionary on us young ministers. This man, A. W. Bailey, had been a pioneer missionary in Africa for forty years. He had accomplished his lifelong objective of establishing mission stations across the width of Africa before retiring. He was a lovely, gracious old man when he was with us, but what surprised us most was how mentally sharp and flexible he was. He seemed to appreciate greatly the opportunity to learn new things from the Scripture and was constantly growing rather than coasting. His closeness to the Lord was apparent right up to his final moments on earth. Eighty-three years old, he was reading Scripture with his wife when he quietly slipped into the presence of the Savior, who was no stranger to him. Many times since then I have prayed that I, too, might walk straight through life with Jesus and into his glorious presence like that!

What Shall We Do?
It is always much easier to spot the harmful effects of enculturation in others than in ourselves. We tend to feel that it is so much a part of our identity that looking for it is like trying to look into our own eyeballs. We do have resources, however. Not only is enculturation a potential danger to new covenant living, but the reverse is true, too. Having new covenant fellowship with the living God is protection from harmful enculturation! There is great flexibility of life that is developed by fellowship with him. There is a different source of security and an excitement in stepping out into new paths to which he calls us.

If we learn to enthrone the Holy Spirit of God in our lives, and by his help draw on the victory of Jesus, we will grow in our ability to sense the Spirit's conviction about anything that blocks or displeases him in our lives. Without this ministry we will be helplessly bound by our enculturations. Walk with him; grow with him; trust him for all the ministries you need. This is not walking on eggs; this is freedom. And the joy of the Lord is your strength!

Valuable Enculturation

A walk with the Spirit of God, with steady attention to his Word and prayer, at the same time that it maintains our flexibility of life, will also establish some of the positive and beneficial enculturations of Christianity. The "forming of Christ" within us, the building of Christian character and integrity, ought not to be a flighty or ephemeral thing—now we have it and now we don't! Rather it should be built deeply into our lives, established there by a day-by-day conditioning process. Even our right faith responses can become more habitual and skillful!

My wife is a first-grade teacher in a Christian school, and she, along with many other Christian teachers, has noticed that children "are just not what they used to be." Where certain traits of character, such as respect for authority, taking of responsibility for actions and trustworthiness once made children from Christian families the stabilizing center for discipline in their classrooms, this is no longer as often observed. No doubt many pressures have been operating on them to condition them in a different and destructive pattern.

Young people today seem to bring with them into their marriages fewer of the character traits that promote solid hope for good marriages. Here, too, the problem of how to enculturate valuable character traits is a serious concern for thoughtful Christians.

The renewal of the church, brought about by a new outcropping of new covenant living, must reach into the warp and woof of Christian culture to produce believers who are able to walk humbly and flexibly with their God, while exhibiting rock-ribbed integrity of character. Our day cries out for such people! And at the risk of sounding like I am grossly oversimplifying the matter, I want to assure you that if you concentrate on growth in fellowship with the Spirit of God, you will make a profound contribution to this renewal.

CHAPTER 14

SEPARATISM

If you are a student of human nature, you know that people who say they always prefer to be alone have conflicts inside. They were created social beings. If they are out of contact with people and do not enjoy their company, some combination of pressures has confirmed them in their loneliness. Like everyone else, they really desire to be known, understood and cared for, and they hurt when there is a lack of these things in their lives. They also know, at least subconsciously, that they need to give these gifts to others.

But life has stumped them somehow. Perhaps they have come to fear people. Perhaps they think they are so ugly that people will naturally turn away from them. Perhaps they have a physical affliction and find social amenities quite painful and embarrassing. Perhaps they have been badly hurt by people and are not about to chance a repeat of that. Whatever the reason, they are confirmed loners.

In the light of biblical teaching about God's plan to draw all things together in Christ and create a united humanity, we know that something is seriously wrong when Christians divide. We as Christians have two conflicting tendencies where relationships are concerned. We have indeed been created by God with the capacity and need to interact with him and with our fellow human beings. But the intrusion of sin into our nature has created a push toward independence. We have to face the fact that there is something in us that will drive us toward aloneness, if it is not brought under control.

I have struggled to find the right name for this tendency. *Independency* doesn't quite cover it, although it is close. *Autonomy*, being subject to no one but ourself, is part of it. *Self-centeredness* is involved. I want a word that will stand in contrast with the heart of the new covenant reality of *union:* union with Christ on a personal, individual level and union with him on a corporate level. *Individualism* almost does it, but is awkward to use in describing a corporate display of party spirit.

The idea really centers in our tendency to be separate, rather than united, and therefore the word *separatism* would be useful. The problem is that this word has a couple of rather narrow uses, and I want to use it broadly. People who emphasize certain ways of being distinct from the world often speak of *separation*, and what they are advocating could be called *separatism*. That is not what I have in mind. Separatism is also used to describe a withdrawal of whole groups of Christians from other Christians for the sake of avoiding compromise with false doctrine or worldliness. In some circumstances I might be including that meaning, but I also want to cover much more. If you will just bear in mind that I am talking about all the levels at which our flesh is antagonistic toward our union with Christ and other Christians, we can understand each other. Whatever name is given to it, this is a significant roadblock to new covenant lifestyle.

Separatism, then, directly confronts and attacks the heart of new covenant mystery: individual union with Jesus Christ and union with each other in him. At the center of covenant truth is our fellowship with God. This is what covenants are designed to bring about and maintain. In the case of the new covenant, Jesus has done such a work that the Spirit of God now indwells his human temples in a more intimate fellowship than had ever been possible before. It is the high culmination, at least to this point in history, of God's desire and design to be with his people. And as we share together that intimate presence of the Spirit, this is the high culmination of God's desire and design to produce an integrated society.

Separatism and Individual Fellowship with God

The separatist tendency can subtly mar your relationship with God. As a unique individual you have been created with a variety of gifts and strengths. It is probably at the point of their greatest strengths that most Christians face their strongest temptation to go it alone. If you are specially gifted mentally, you will want to trust your own understanding and operate without a functioning intellectual fellowship with the Holy Spirit. This will become increasingly true as you engage in disciplined training of your mind. After all, you have worked hard to obtain a trustworthy instrument, and you surely are entitled to trust your independent use of it. If you have a large emotional capacity, you will easily desire to keep your feelings as your private reserve and shut the Holy Spirit out of them. If you are strong willed, you will find it that much harder to exercise your choices and determinations in a submitted relationship to the Holy Spirit. Your strongest appetites will be the places where you are most sorely tempted to self-gratification. These strengths were intended to be great blessings to you, but their true value is lost when they function out of fellowship with God.

Cultural surroundings may encourage personal separatism. In America a cult is made of self-sufficiency and individual accomplishments. In pop psychology, all roads seem to start or end with a good self-image and self-love—good insights but dangerous without new covenant teaching. Materialism worms its way into our American lifestyle and creates self-centeredness.

The experiences of our lives—the abuses, hurts and tragedies we have suffered—easily tend to make us want to withdraw into ourselves. Sometimes this even causes us to fear trusting God and opening our lives to him. There can be resulting bondages of fear or overdependence on human beings or structures, and this blights fellowship with God. A wide variety of causes can push toward separatism.

We need to recognize this thrust for what it is. The sin that is in our nature, even as Christians, has this character. This will be a central obstacle to our walk with the Holy Spirit. When he helps us realize that our fellowship isn't what it ought to be—that we have been drifting out of step—let us recognize what has happened. Our flesh wants to draw back from God.

Praise God that our union with Christ and his victory, along with the presence of the Holy Spirit to administer it, provide us with all the resources we need to deal with the separatist tendency in ourselves. Ask the Holy Spirit's help; choose to die with Christ to your right to be independent; honor the Holy Spirit as your Companion; invite him to have fellowship with you in your thinking, your feelings, your will, your appetites. In Jesus' name command the devil to get off your back. If there are specific sins that God makes you conscious of, confess them, but by all means do more than that. Claim the healing of your fellowship by the instruments Christ has made available to you.

Separatism and Fellowship with Other Christians

We Christians are often preoccupied with individual progress in grace. Even the architecture of our churches often hinders fellowship. Chances are good that your church auditorium is a long narrow room where you can see no one but the minister and the choir if you are in the front row, and the backs of 399 heads if you are in the last row. Such a design seems ingeniously contrived to eliminate group consciousness, making it possible for 400 people to be in the same place without being together. This wouldn't be so commonplace if there weren't something in human nature that wants it that way.

In displaying these tendencies, we betray our failure to understand new covenant realities. Those people in church are, for the most part, our brothers and sisters in Christ. We are in permanent union with them. From this base the new covenant teaches love, care, encouragement, servanthood, interaction of gifts, and mutual glorifying of Christ. The Bible talks of addressing each other in psalms, hymns and spiritual songs. It talks of two or more agreeing together about what they should ask God. We rightly infer that there is a unique way of knowing Christ when we are together in such functions.

The new covenant mystery of Christ centers around union with him *and* with each other. We ought not to emphasize the one without the other, yet that is just what we often do. But Scripture instructs us both to enter our closets for secret prayer and to pray in harmony with others. We are to grow individually, and we are to grow with others. We are instructed to give and to receive help and encouragement, and we are to work together with other Christians.

We do not achieve a practical unity easily. It is the nature of our flesh to fear, envy, dominate or withdraw. Fits of jealousy and anger easily cause division. A poor self-image will indeed damage unity. So will passions or lusts. It is easy to misunderstand what others say and do. Our flesh can even subtly *want* to find out that others have been malicious or unloving toward us. *"I expected that,"* it mutters gleefully.

How important to discover the power available in Christ for making our union with other Christians practical! The Holy Spirit *is* able to subdue our divisive flesh. In its place he can pour into our lives, directly from Christ himself, the miracles of love, forgiveness, kindness, patience, boldness, care. He can help us take wise actions when divisions threaten, to move toward our brothers and sisters instead of away, to become open and vulnerable toward others as fellowship grows.

Separatism and Larger Group Relationships
Because you belong to a church, a denomination, and perhaps various parachurch organizations, we need to see that the characteristic sins that afflict us as individuals also have group expressions. The groups you are in can be tempted as a group, can go on corporate ego trips, can be divisive or hateful or jealous. Separatism

can function here in a negative way, too. This is often the offense of denominationalism and the tragic fragmentation shown by Christianity to a watching world.

Worshiping and ministering in separate groupings can be quite legitimate. Language barriers, for example, may dictate this. It may even be quite legitimate to separate into denominations over distinctively different modes of worship, baptism or church government. There will be occasions when groups will need to separate in order to preserve sound doctrine and practice. In any of these legitimate situations, however, we do well to watch carefully for the wrong kind of separatism, the kind that elevates distinctives to the point where unchristian behavior is excused, where genuine believers are no longer accepted as true members of Christ's body, where love is displayed only to those who are a part of us. We are then swept along by group passions that make it almost impossible to recognize the Holy Spirit in others.

The acrimony and hatred that can exist between groups of true believers in Christ is frightening. Group will treat group in ways that would make individuals feel quite guilty if they did such things on a one-to-one basis. Yet it is not likely that a group will accept conviction from God's Spirit over its actions and make group confession. We must learn to do this. The same principles that apply to individual growth in sanctification need a corporate expression. At any rate, we should learn to spot the negative energizing of separatism. Legitimate groupings of Christ's people have corporate gifts that can interact with those of other groups. Believe this, and look for ways to serve each other with love and fruit.

GETTING IT
TOGETHER

What have we seen on the journey through this book? We started by looking at a God who loves to make covenants with his people, because he desires fellowship with them. We looked at the old Mosaic covenant which pointed toward Jesus, at Jesus himself the great covenant-keeper, and at the way the new covenant emerged in the apostolic period. We saw the elevation of life this makes possible in the experience of prayer, of victory over evil, of guidance into God's will, and of unity. In the last section we looked at some of the roadblocks which hinder such an experience of the new covenant: an incomplete message, materialism, legalism, enculturation and separatism. We have sought to describe the doctrinal foundation on which to build an elevated experience of new covenant power in fellowship with God.

Our Heavenly Father desires ongoing fellowship with us. The Son has promised never to leave us through the end of the age. His Spirit has been given to abide with us forever. The spiritual structure of redemption in which this communion takes place is always around us, whatever our circumstances.

It will be good for us to keep a few final thoughts in our minds, that we may grow in the reality of all this.

Knowing Jesus and His Spirit

It is no slight to the Father to emphasize the place of Jesus and the Holy Spirit in new covenant fellowship. The Trinity is such that we discern all of God in any of the divine Persons. Jesus, however, has a special centrality in the new covenant. It was he, the second Person of the Godhead, who came to earth and became the last Adam. It was he who represented us in his obedience, in his covenant-keeping, and in his great work of redemption. It was through his death that our marriage to evil has been dissolved, and it is in his resurrection life that we are made alive in the new marriage. He is the One making claim for us and supplying the Holy Spirit to us from the Father and himself. He is the head of the body, the victor over all our ills, the holder of our life purpose, the source of our gifts, and the creator of our union with himself and with other Christians. He is alive and real!

When Paul talked about being Jesus' slave, about his earnest desire to *know* Christ, his deep commitment to please him—when he said that for him to live was Christ—he voiced the kind of faith that is available to all believers under the new covenant. The living Christ was real to his eye of faith, and he can be to ours, too. Although Jesus is invisible to our physical eyes, he can be so real to us that it is as though we see him. This is exactly the way Hebrews states it: "But we see Jesus . . . now crowned with glory and honor" (2:9 NIV). The same writer says "fix your thoughts on Jesus, the apostle and high priest whom we confess" (3:1 NIV).

This seeing by faith can be so strong, his reality, glory and love so captivating, that we come to love him as we love no other being. I doubt that anyone can improve on the King James rendering of Peter's thoughts along this line: "Whom having not seen, ye love; in whom, though now ye see him not, yet believing, ye rejoice with joy unspeakable and full of glory" (1 Pet 1:8). Knowing Jesus in this way will make it ever so much easier to respond with the kind of faith that will open up the privileges of new covenant living.

In a similar way we may have communion with the Holy Spirit. Jesus told his disciples, "You *know* him, for he lives with you and will be in you" (Jn 14:17 NIV). Only as we know the Holy Spirit can we fully know and exalt Jesus. The Holy Spirit is God, indwelling us at the deepest level of our lives. Anyone who teaches that the Holy Spirit does not want to be personally known and loved, needs to confront the fact that he is God—fully God, the self-revealing God. He desires to be known, loved and understood as he lives with us. In his presence God's covenant design to establish fellowship with himself is most intimately achieved. In knowing him, we will know the Father and the Son better.

For our limited minds, the mystery of the Trinity and the marvel of knowing God perhaps are best understood through the appreciation we develop for the unique functions of each member of the Godhead. We know Jesus in his redemptive work and unique functions as the Man, so it is also through the unique functions ascribed to the Holy Spirit as our Helper and Indweller that we come to know him. We grow in awareness of him as we experience the things he has come to do in us. We can ask, expect, know and love him in the doing of these things. In any case, we will grow greatly as our eye of faith sees him.

Using the Bible

In order for our eye of faith to become sharper in seeing Jesus and his Spirit, we will need the repeated impact of Scriptures on our hearts. "We conclude that faith is awakened by the message, and the message that awakens it comes through the word of Christ" (Rom 10:17 NEB).

Remember what the central role of Scripture is. It is more than a source of propositional truth *about* God and redemption. It is more than a collection of rules for Old Testament and New Testament ethics. It is God's means of revealing himself and bringing us into relationship with himself. Covenant and canon are the same, and both exist to build and maintain fellowship with God. The fact that new covenant privileges became the center and initiation of New

Testament Scriptures, indicates at once God's intention to use these revelations to build the new intimacy with Christ and his Spirit.

This should clearly indicate the kind of approach to take toward the Bible. We begin with prayer and depend on the Holy Spirit to use the Word in our hearts to quicken our faith and enable us to make the right responses to Christ and him.

Obviously the new covenant writings will be specially meaningful to us. But as the New Testament has its full impact on us, we will find a great thing happening. We will find that the Old Testament Scriptures also add to our new covenant experiences. This is really not so strange. The Old Testament is covenant, too. It too involved the grace of God toward his people and his desire and design to be in fellowship with them. It is true that a veil was over the scene then, but now that veil has been lifted. The mystery previously hidden is hidden no more. We will find all that God has said to be effective in drawing us into worship, praise and fellowship with him. We will find that the Old Testament is full of Jesus Christ, too. The new covenant opens up the old and draws it into one mighty instrument of new covenant grace. New covenant people become whole-Bible people in a way never before possible, and the eye of faith is greatly strengthened.

An Active Life

Perhaps you are inclined to think that with all this emphasis on the completed work of Christ and his intercession for us in the new covenant framework, our part will be mostly that of resting and watching to see what God will do—basically a passive lifestyle.

The very nature of *fellowship* should make us uneasy with that idea. God wants people who will walk with him, who will interact with him mentally, emotionally and in their choices. Passivity is not a characteristic of true fellowship.

The Scripture cuts squarely across all notions of passivity. Though Christ has completed the work and now lays claim to the results of it, you are called on to enter into the chain of intercession by praying earnestly in the Spirit. This is a picture of powerful prayer activity, not contrary to new covenant privileges, but entering right into the heart of them. You are called on to wage a strong fight against sin, to resist the devil in the authority of Christ, to overcome the world. This is to be done, not apart from new covenant connections, but in the virtue and power of that very union.

You are called on to understand what the will of the Lord is, to guard your trust by the Holy Spirit, to walk in the light. You are called on to keep the unity of the Spirit in the bond of peace. In doing these things you can be moving in harmony with the Holy Spirit as he moves in your heart. There is the strong call of Scripture to step out by faith, not independently, but in a vigorous walk with God. You are to be released to be everything that God designed you to be. Abiding in Christ the covenant-keeper, you have the strongest possible assurance that your prayer claims and subsequent activities are to be powerfully effective.

When Things Don't Seem to Be Happening

You may often feel that you have been led by these truths to step out into large claims of prayer and expectation. Then you may face discouragement when results don't seem to measure up to what you hoped for. There is real danger that your discouragement could lead you back into passivity. You may even entertain a deep-down feeling that God has let you down.

But God has not let you down! He cannot let you down, because he cannot let his Son down, and you are in Jesus. You must stand on the fact of his absolute dependability and response *on the ground of the covenant*. Don't rely on your feelings. Don't let yourself get drawn into the trap of measuring God's performance by your expectations, but rather seek to grow steadily in fellowship with him. You must, by the Holy Spirit's help, maintain the activity of faith and the good works that Christ has planned for you, regardless of what you see or experience that seems negative. This is vigorous fellowship with the Spirit of Christ, who never deserts us.

Renewing the Church

Many Christians today are praying earnestly for revival and renewal in the church. You have perhaps read stirring accounts of past movements of the Holy Spirit which came with sweeping power. Even non-Christians were seized with an overwhelming sense of the reality and holiness of God. I, too, long for such displays of God's sovereign power.

Perhaps we have tended to feel that no really significant renewal of the church can take place until such a sovereign display of God's power is granted. But just think for a moment of what kinds of things would become true in Christ's church, if the new covenant privileges described in this book were more widely experienced. Jesus Christ is right now engaged in active intercession for us. The Holy Spirit is already moving in powerful ways, both in individuals and in his body. God has made possible a display by his people of their fellowship with the glorious Christ that can surely outshine anything seen in the church before—a level of transformation from glory to glory *already provided for* in our Savior. The kind of life opened up to us by the new covenant is no small display of life and power. Perhaps the picture of a united, victorious and guided church, operating by new covenant prayer, would look remarkably like one of the greatest revivals the church has ever known.

At any rate, you can make a strong contribution toward renewal by your own response to these truths.

May the King of kings, the great covenant-keeper, in his living glory, transform you by his Spirit, and reign wonderfully in his kingdom. Let us walk with him!

Appendix

PAUL'S LIFE AND THE DATE OF GALATIANS

It is probably not possible to be as precise as we would like to be in setting up a chronology of apostolic times. However, Paul's life, as described in Acts and in his letters, provides a wealth of data, and there are significant interactions with events in nonbiblical history.

Part one of this book treats Paul's letter to the Galatians as the first New Testament writing. Scholars do not agree on the date for Galatians, and many would contest my supposition. It is not a novel suggestion, however, and certainly not a theory which can be disproved easily. In this Appendix, I will reproduce for those interested in chronological studies the manner in which I became personally convinced of Galatians' lead-off position.

Assuming the unity and integrity of the New Testament canon, I begin with the chronological notices found in Paul's letters and the book of Acts and work to fit this data with extrabiblical evidence.

We will first build a proposed chronology of Paul's life from his conversion through the first 17 or 18 years of his Christian experience and ministry. We will do this by pinpointing three times when events in extrabiblical history intersect with biblical accounts and so create a framework within which events can be estimated. Then we shall seek to evaluate what this does to the date of Galatians. At worst we will find the early date for Galatians possible, at best probable.

Establishing a Chronology

1. *Death of Herod Agrippa in A.D. 44 and the famine visit of Paul and Barnabas to Jerusalem.* The arrest of Peter and his deliverance from prison, recorded in Acts 12, is described as happening during the Feast of Unleavened Bread just before Passover. In A.D. 44 this was the first week in May. Agrippa's death, according to Josephus, occurred in connection with a festival honoring the Emperor Claudius, possibly his birthday, August 1. At any rate, the year 44 for Agrippa's death is one of the better-established dates in history, and so we consider it first.

At the end of Acts 11, Luke records the prophecy by Agabus that a worldwide famine was coming and then records that it came during Emperor Claudius's reign. The Antioch church took up a relief offering for the Jerusalem Christians and sent it to Jerusalem by the hand of Barnabas and Paul (Acts 11:29-30). The last verse of Acts 12 records the return of Barnabas and Paul to Antioch after fulfilling their mission. Thus the events of chapter 12, including Agrippa's death, are inserted in the text by Luke between the notices of arrival and departure of the messengers from Antioch.

The most natural assumption would be that Barnabas and Paul made this trip to Jerusalem in A.D. 44 about the time of the Acts 12 events. This runs into some difficulty with Josephus's account, however. Josephus records a famine occurring in Jerusalem during the rule of the successive Roman procurators, Fadus and Alexander. Fadus came into office after Agrippa's death, so that it would seem that A.D. 45 would be the earliest date for the famine in Josephus's account. This is not a large discrepancy, however. Famines do not arrive suddenly and full-blown, and the Antioch church had had early warning of it through Agabus. It would seem entirely plausible that Barnabas and Paul were in Jerusalem during some part of A.D. 44. This date then becomes a reasonably secure point in Paul's chronology.

By the help of Acts 11:26 we can now suggest a date for Paul's arrival at Antioch. That verse states that Barnabas found Paul in Tarsus and brought him to Antioch, then: "So for a whole year Barnabas and Saul met with the church and taught great numbers of people" (NIV). This suggests A.D. 43 for Paul's arrival in Antioch.

Acts 13 records the initiation of the first missionary journey as the next event after the famine trip, so we may feel secure in placing it in A.D. 45. Our chronology now looks like this:

A.D. 43 End Paul's silent years; Barnabas gets Saul

A.D. 43-44 Ministry in Antioch

A.D. 44 Famine relief trip to Jerusalem

A.D. 45 First missionary trip begins

2. *Paul's escape from Damascus while its governor was under King Aretas.* In 2 Co-

rinthian 11:32-33, Paul describes his exciting escape from Damascus: "In Damascus the governor under King Aretas had the city of the Damascenes guarded in order to arrest me. But I was lowered in a basket from a window in the wall and slipped through his hands" (NIV). Aretas was a name something like "Herod" in the sense that it applied to successive kings, who ruled the Nabatean Arabs. The king referred to here was Aretas IV. Much of the time Damascus was ruled directly by the Romans, but they apparently turned over the active rule of Damascus to Aretas IV sometime in the mid 30s. Some scholars think this change may have occurred as early as A.D. 34; others place the change at A.D. 37, coinciding with the ascendancy of Caligula as Roman emperor. This latter date is reinforced by the appearance of Aretan coins in Damascus replacing Roman coins around A.D. 37. We can easily conjecture that the change in rule over Damascus may have made Paul's ministry there dramatically more dangerous, whereas under the Romans he had had relative safety.

If A.D. 37 is the correct time for Aretas IV to have gained control of Damascus, Paul's escape could not have been earlier than that year. Galatians 1:18 indicates that the total stay of Paul in Damascus was three years, including the time spent apart in "Arabia." Thus if his escape took place in A.D. 37 or 38, all or most of three years would take us back to A.D. 35 for his conversion. We are now able to suggest the following enlarged chronology:

A.D. 35 Paul's conversion en route to Damascus
A.D. 35-37 Ministry in Damascus plus Arabian retreat
A.D. 37/38 Escape from Damascus; trip to Jerusalem
A.D. 38-43 Silent years of ministry around Tarsus
A.D. 43 Barnabas gets Paul
A.D. 43-44 Ministry in Antioch
A.D. 44 Famine relief trip to Jerusalem
A.D. 45 First missionary trip begins

3. *Paul at Corinth on 2nd missionary trip—Gallio proconsul.* Here we come to a pivotal point in establishing a chronology of Paul's life and ministry. Acts 18:12-17 describes a united attack by the Jews upon Paul at Corinth, "When Gallio was proconsul of Achaia" (verse 12 NIV). An inscription at Delphi gives specific information regarding the year-long period of Gallio's rule in Corinth. It says that he was proconsul during the twelfth year of the Emperor Claudius's tribunicial power and after his twenty-sixth proclamation as emperor. The twenty-seventh such proclamation occurred by August A.D. 52, so Gallio's year must have begun before that date. Usually proconsuls took office in midsummer. Scholars are divided over whether Gallio's year went from the summer of A.D. 51 to summer of A.D. 52, or was one year later. If the earlier year is assumed, then Paul's brush with

him would have taken place before midsummer A.D. 52. The text in Acts seems to describe a sequence of ministries in Corinth before the Gallio incident, and perhaps implies that the confrontation occurred early in Gallio's rule. These factors could push the beginning of Paul's eighteen-month ministry in Corinth back into A.D. 50. This really leaves too little time for the 1200-mile journey, with multiple ministries along the way, which brought Paul to Corinth. It would seem more likely that Paul arrived in Corinth in A.D. 51 and came before Gallio perhaps a year later in A.D. 52. If it is actually important to have this incident take place early in Gallio's rule, then the later year for Gallio's term would be necessary. If not, then either would do. In any case, we fix Paul's visit to Corinth in A.D. 51 and 52.

Now we are in a position to work backward toward the last date set in our chronology. We first must allow enough time for Paul to get to Corinth on this second missionary trip. Apparently Paul and Silas set out from Antioch soon after the great Council in Jerusalem described in Acts 15. Their first labors were to strengthen the churches in Syria and Cilicia. These are presumably churches established by Paul during his silent years of ministry (see Gal 1:21-23; Acts 15:23, 41). Then they went on to the South Galatian churches established during the first journey (Acts 16:1-5). Here they went from town to town delivering the Council decrees. After this the account describes a journey right across the province of Asia, with strong constraints from the Lord against ministering in this area (16:6-8). Crossing into Macedonia they had rapid ministries in Philippi, Thessalonica, Berea and Athens before coming to Corinth. Allowing perhaps three to six months for the initial revisiting of churches, two to three months actual travel time for the whole trip, and three or four months for the ministries just prior to Corinth, we must assume that, rapid as it was, this trip must have consumed the best part of a year to bring Paul to Corinth. This reckoning would place the Acts 15 Jerusalem Council perhaps early in A.D. 50.

Coming forward from the last item in our previous list, we had the first missionary journey beginning in A.D. 45. Tucked away in the account of that trip are many inconspicuous notices that really compel us to allow a fair amount of time for that ministry (note, for example, Acts 13:6; 13:49; 14:3, 6, 21-23). Three years would seem none too much. The rest of the time until the Council at Jerusalem would have been spent basically back in Antioch, two momentous years of crisis.

Now our chronology looks like this:

A.D. 35 Paul's conversion en route to Damascus
A.D. 35-37 Ministry in Damascus plus Arabian retreat
A.D. 37/38 Escape from Damascus; trip to Jerusalem

A.D. 38-43 Silent years of ministry around Tarsus
A.D. 43 Barnabas gets Paul
A.D. 43-44 Ministry in Antioch
A.D. 44 Famine relief trip to Jerusalem
A.D. 45-48 First missionary trip begins
A.D. 48-50 Crisis period based at Antioch
A.D. 50 Council at Jerusalem
A.D. 50-51 Second journey as far as Corinth
A.D. 51-52 Stay at Corinth

This is as far as we need to take Paul's life for our present purposes. We next want to consider the date of Galatians.

The Date of Writing Galatians

It is the suggestion of this book that Galatians was the very first of the New Testament writings and that it was written about A.D. 49.

For this to be true we have to adhere to what is known as the South Galatian theory as opposed to the North Galatian theory regarding the destination of this letter. This is partly a geographical problem. There was a time when it was thought incorrect to describe the cities visited in the first missionary journey—Derbe, Lystra, Iconium, and so forth—as *Galatian* at all. They were considered to be south and outside of Galatia. Considerable research and scholarly work has shown that these cities may indeed be designated properly as Galatian (for a review of this debate see Donald Guthrie, *New Testament Introduction* [Downers Grove, Ill.: InterVarsity Press, 1970], pp. 450-57).

Many factors make the South Galatian theory preferable. For one thing, the supposition often made in connection with the North Galatian theory that the establishing of these churches took place during the second missionary journey as Paul and Silas made their way westward toward the province of Asia seems highly unlikely. No mention is made of such a ministry by Luke, and this would be most uncharacteristic of him. There also does not seem to be adequate time available to squeeze such an extensive ministry into that trip. On the other hand, many characteristics of the crisis in the church that occurred during the late 40s make the South Galatian destination very attractive.

Both the South Galatian destination for Paul's letter and its early date fit well with the historical information in Galatians 1 and 2. The trip by Paul, Barnabas and Titus to Jerusalem to check out their gospel message would have occurred prior to the writing of Galatians and after the first missionary trip. In Galatians 2:1 Paul says about this trip, "Fourteen years later I went up again to Jerusalem" (NIV). From the sequence of events in the latter part of chapter one, this fourteen years could be understood as dating from the end of the Damascus ministry, which in our chronology we have placed in 37 or 38. This would date the trip about A.D. 51 or 52. This is impossible, since we know that Paul was in Corinth at that time. However, if Paul uses the time reference in Galatians 2:1 in the same way he does the time reference in 1:18, we would understand him to be referring back to his conversion in A.D. 35. The fourteen years then would place this trip in A.D. 49, possibly late 48. This would make it soon after the return from the first missionary trip.

Also Peter's visit to Antioch, his good fellowship at first with the Gentile Christians there, the visit by a delegation from James, which apparently included some from the "circumcision party" in Jerusalem, and the ensuing division and confrontation in Antioch between Paul and Peter—all this preceded the writing of Galatians (because recorded there) and fits in the same crucial period after the return from the first trip.

The sequence of events thus might go as follows. The missionary party returns in A.D. 48. After reporting to the church at Antioch, Paul is soon led to make the trip to Jerusalem to check out his gospel with the leaders of the church there. His visit perhaps arouses much interest on the part of the Jerusalem leaders in what is happening at Antioch. Peter decides to visit Antioch (perhaps he even went back with Paul, Barnabas and Silas), and presently a delegation also comes from James. The division and confrontation occur. Perhaps the same group that had come from James, hearing more about the new churches in South Galatia, decide to go on from Antioch around the bend of the Mediterranean Sea to visit those churches. It was only another 125 miles or so. At any rate some group of this sort went there and created the same kind of havoc that had occurred at Antioch. This all occurs in A.D. 49. Paul soon receives word back of the damage done among his converts and writes back to them the anguished letter that we know as Galatians. It is the first New Testament writing and the date is A.D. 49. Soon more representatives of the circumcision party come to Antioch and this time the conflict is so severe that all agree to the calling of the Council in Jerusalem. This takes place perhaps early in A.D. 50.

A compelling line of argument for an early date for Galatians is the absence of any mention of the Jerusalem Council or its action in the letter. The Galatian letter was written to cope with the circumcision/Judaism problem. This also was the problem handled by the Jerusalem Council. The Council basically pronounced in favor of Paul's position. It seems inconceivable that Paul, even if he were addressing a different group of churches five or ten years later, would have failed to make use of the Council's pronouncement. Yet he writes Galatians as though the Council had not met, as though no decrees had been issued. The only satisfactory explanation is that it had indeed not yet met and the dispatch to the mission churches had not yet been issued. It is worth noting that immediately after the Council had met, Paul and Silas headed for those churches to distribute its decrees (Acts 16:4).

Another interesting chronological track which bears on Galatians has to do with Paul's illness. In 2 Corinthians 12 Paul describes the experience of "a man in Christ that I know" who received unspeakable revelations from God. He says that this happened fourteen years before (vv. 2-5). He then lets us in on his circumlocution by admitting that he himself was the one who had been given these remarkable special revelations, and that God had also given him "a thorn in the flesh" to keep him humble. It had tormented him deeply, yet God would not take it away. The date now advocated for the writing of 2 Corinthians is A.D. 57 or perhaps a year earlier. Fourteen years before its writing would bring us back to either A.D. 43 or 42—at the end of Paul's period of silent ministry, just prior to Barnabas's success in relocating him to Antioch. At least the experience of revelations would go in that period; the physical difficulties could have developed somewhat afterward.

The interesting thing is to hear Paul in Galatians describe how he came to them when he first ministered to them: "As you know, it was because of an illness that I first preached the gospel to you. Even though my illness was a trial to you, you did not treat me with contempt or scorn. . . . If you could have done so, you would have torn out your eyes and given them to me" (Gal 4:13-15 NIV). The timing fits the South Galatian destination perfectly.

It is also interesting to see how the historical account given by Paul in Galatians 1 and 2 comes to its climax in the confrontation of Peter by Paul at Antioch and then flows directly into the argument of the letter. That Paul goes no further in his account, even though the Jerusalem Council may have occurred only a short time later, gives one the feeling that the letter came almost immediately after the confrontation with Peter. None of these things are conclusive, but they do create an atmosphere much more congenial to the early date of Galatians than to other theories.

One last note to this appendix, this having to do with Paul's age. He first appears on the scene at the martyrdom of Stephen, where he is called "a young man." According to the lexicons, the word so translated means a man between twenty-four and forty! The fact that he stood in well enough with the Sanhedrin to be immediately commissioned by them to the task of subduing Christians, implies that he may well have been beyond the earlier portion of that age range. He may well have been thirty years old or more. If we give Paul a couple of years for his persecution activities, Stephen's martyrdom may have been something like A.D. 33, and Paul may have been of a chronological age that nearly matches the century years. This would put him in his early forties when Barnabas brought him to Antioch and in his middle sixties when Emperor Nero killed him.

CHRONOLOGY OF APOSTOLIC TIMES

A.D.	Apostolic Events	Paul's Letters	Checkpoints In Secular History
30	Pentecost		
31			
32			
33			
34			
35	Paul's conversion 34 or 35		
36	In Damascus & Arabia		
37	To Jerusalem & Tarsus		Aretus over Damascus
38			(Cf. Acts 9:25 with
39	Silent		2 Cor 11:32-33
40	years of		
41	ministry		
42			
43	Barnabas gets Paul—Antioch		
44	Famine visit to Jerusalem		Death of Herod Agrippa
45	First missionary trip		(Acts 12:23)
46			
47			
48	Return to Antioch and		
49	crisis years	Gal	
50	Jerusalem Council & 2nd		
51	missionary trip—		Gallio in Corinth
52	Paul at Corinth	1, 2 Thess	A.D. 51 & 52
53			(Cf. Acts 18:12)
54	3rd missionary trip		
55	Long stay at Ephesus	1 Cor	
56		2 Cor	
57	Macedonia & Achaia	Romans	
58	To Jerusalem—Arrest		
59	(held in Palestine)		
60	Prison in Rome	Eph Col	
61		Philippians	
62		Philemon	
63	Release, further trips		
64			Fire in Rome—Nero
65		1 Tim Tit	begins to persecute
66	2nd prison time in Rome	2 Tim	Christians
67	Paul's death in Rome		
68	(prob. Peter's too)		Death of Nero